more weird sports

Sol Neelman

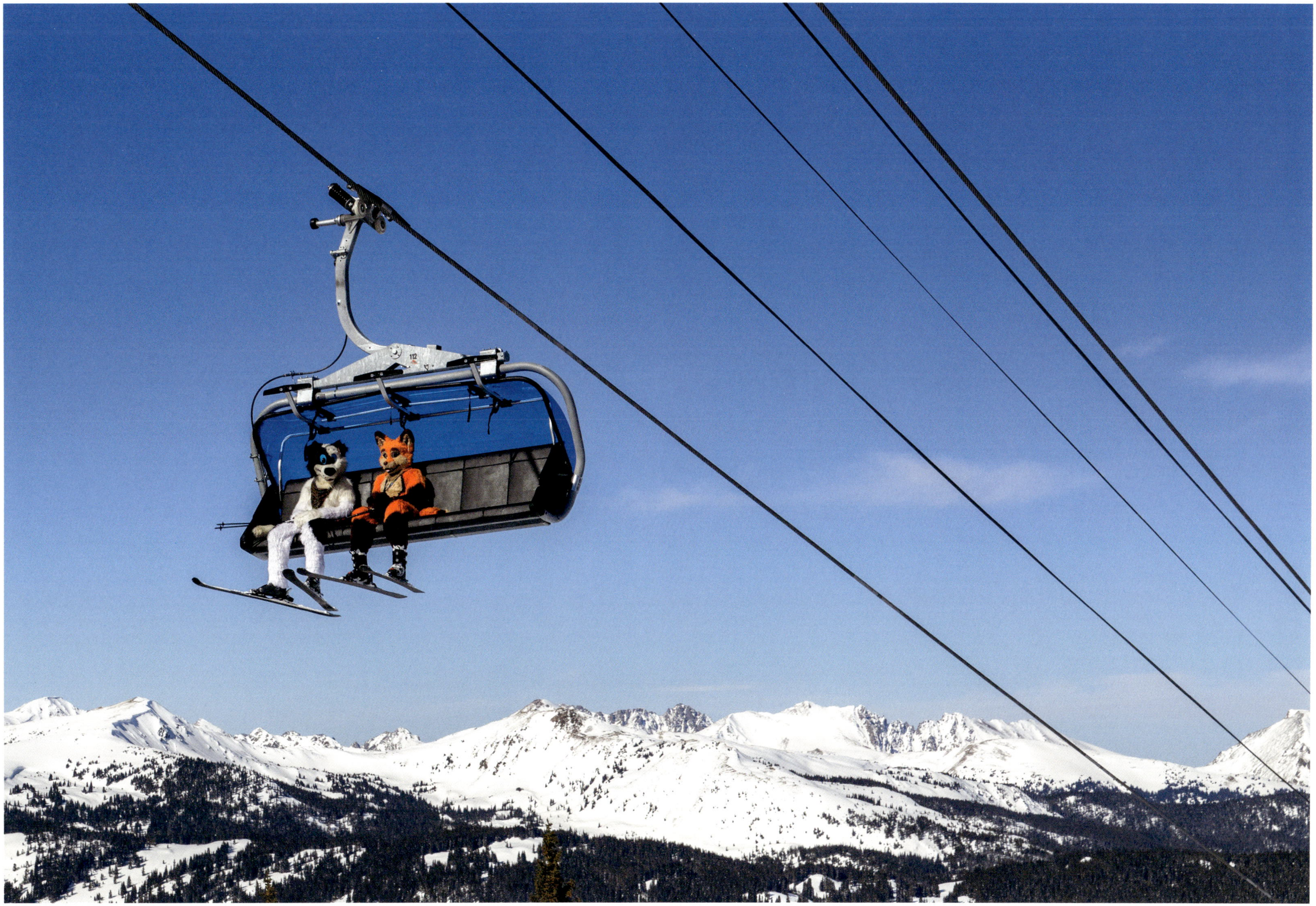

Furry Ski Weekend

Copper Mountain, Colorado, USA

KEHRER

Sol Neelman

more weird sports

The Foreword

If there is nothing else you get from this compilation of joyful weirdness ("i before e except when it's WEIRD" as Sol likes to remind me), I want you to envision Sol Neelman's laughing face as he stares wide-eyed through a camera at 500 English lunatics tumbling down a mountain after a wheel of cheese.

The thing most non-photographers don't consider about a photo is how much of it is affected by the person behind the lens and how they show up to the moment in that image. What you need to know about this mensch Sol Neelman is that if he shows up with a camera in your face, there's a good goddamned chance that you'll be laughing in the photo.

I have a long hallway in my house. There are about seven images hanging on the wall that Sol took at my wedding. Every time someone new visits, they linger on those images. They laugh, they ask about the moments and the people in them. Pretty much everyone comments on what an amazingly fun wedding it must have been. There is so much joy and play in those photos.

So here's the thing about that wedding: It was fun. Lots of tears, lots of laughter. But I gotta tell you that I'm about 95 percent sure it wasn't as fun as Sol's pictures. I'll give you an example: We were in an orchard. Sol grabbed a ladder from a barn and climbed it, surrounded by apple trees. He gathered everyone in a tight formation for a big picture. Pretty standard, right? Once he checked that group photo off the list, he climbed down and walked toward the group. Camera shutter at full throttle, Sol walked slowly in and out of this tight group, making fun of me, cracking jokes with everyone, yelling broken

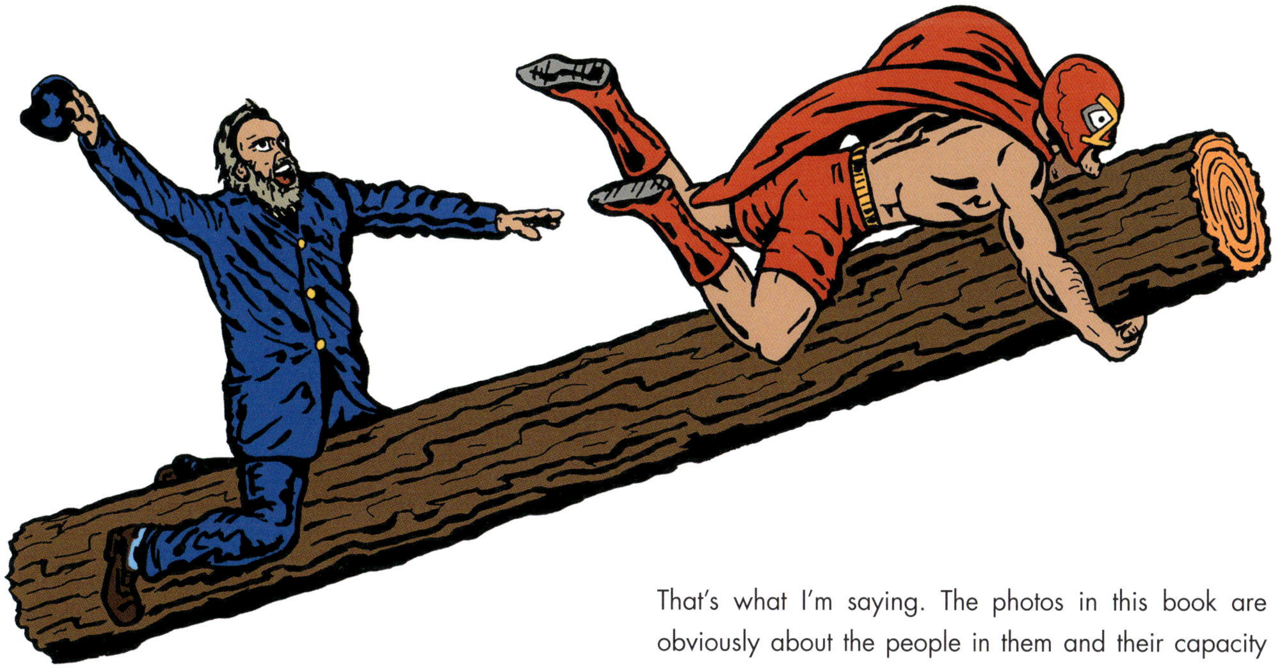

Spanish to my Mexican family, asking provocative questions and making everyone double over in laughter. From my 75-year-old mom to my 9-year-old nephew, everyone was in fits of laughter. We have images completely full of 35 faces expressing every variation of joy and happiness you can imagine. It was pure Sol—looking for connection, bringing out our joy and deepening our love.

That's what I'm saying. The photos in this book are obviously about the people in them and their capacity for delight and their love of community. But they are also inevitably about Sol and how he makes people feel when he comes into their space.

For me, one of the cool things about reviewing someone's photos is gaining an insight into what they value, what they love, what moments matter to them. For a lot of us, it's one of the more challenging things about showing the world our creative work. For better or worse, we are in that work. In many ways, we are that work.

These photos are Sol. They capture people doing silly things they love with people they love. They don't do it for money, or status, or fame. They do it for the community, the absurdity, and the laughter. Weird Sports is, like the events it lovingly chronicles, a celebration of authenticity and individuality. If the cliché is true and sports act as a metaphor for life, Sol's choice of sports metaphor tells you everything about his values: The only weird thing about these sports is that they're so pared down to this vital place where competition remains secondary to joy, and deepening friendships is both the reason to play and the goal of the game.

David Noles
Amateur log rider, fresh bagel Sherpa and the Jay-Z of Brooklyn portrait photography

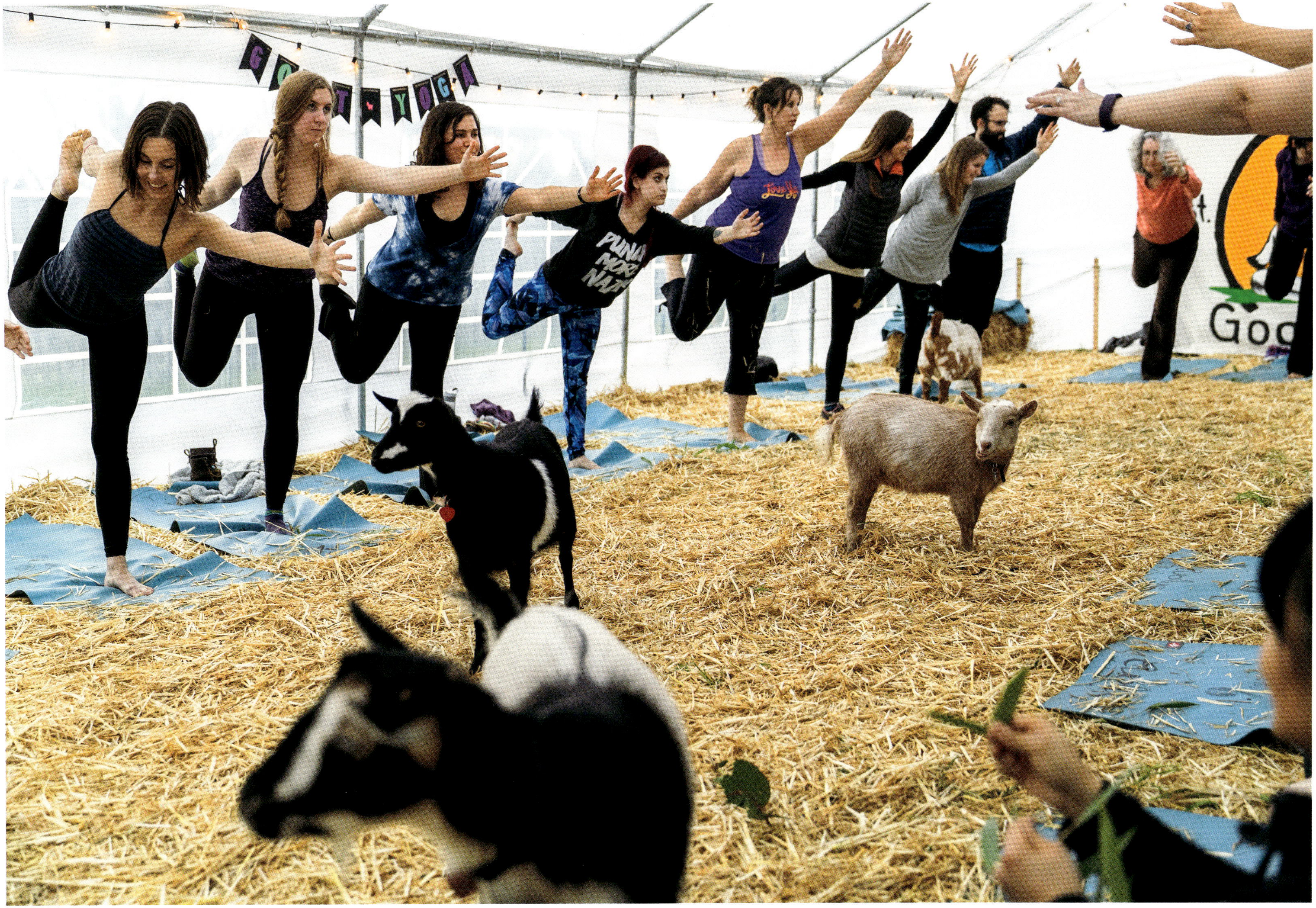

Goat Yoga

Corvallis, Oregon, USA

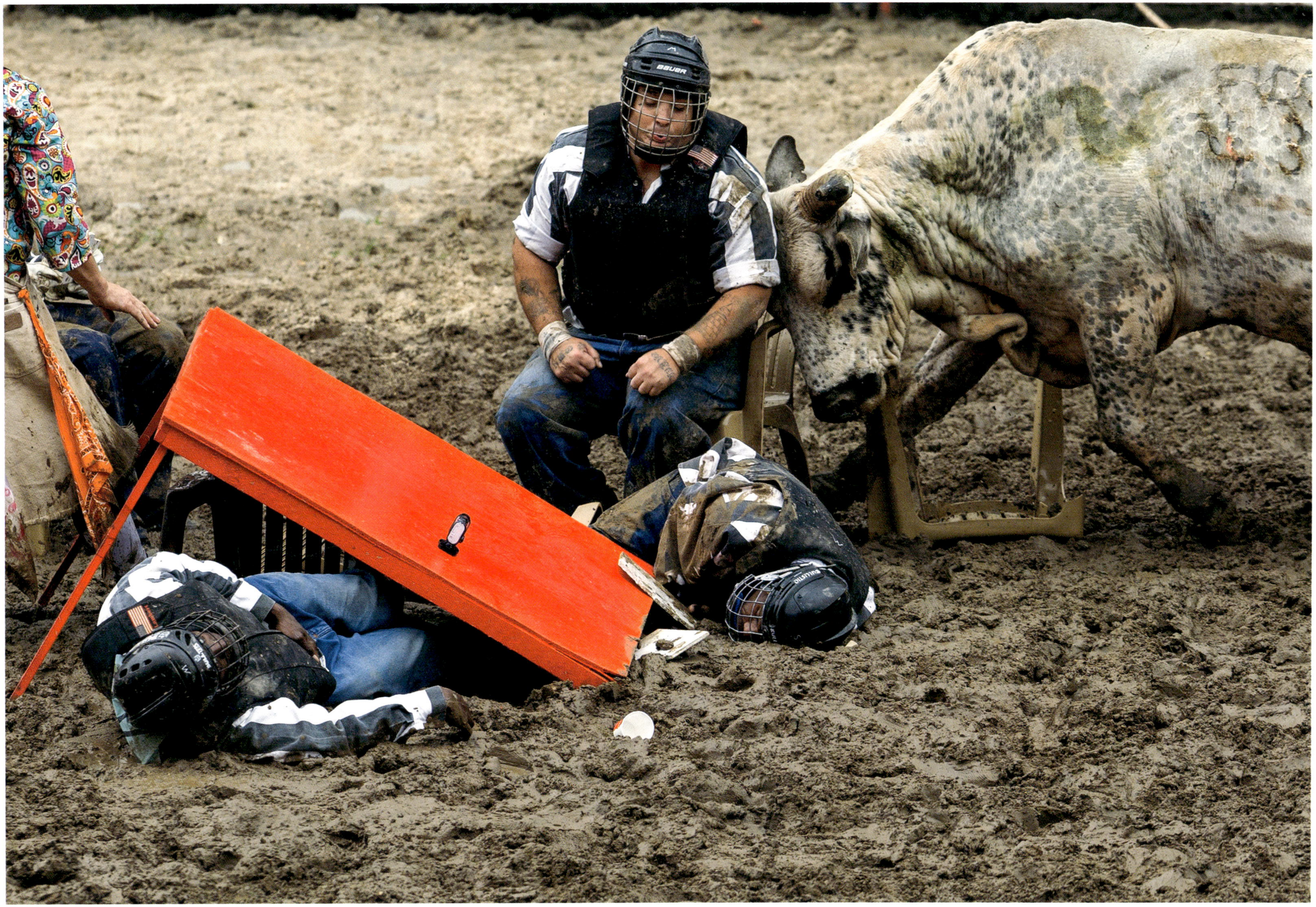

Convict Poker

Louisiana State Penitentiary, Angola, Louisiana, USA

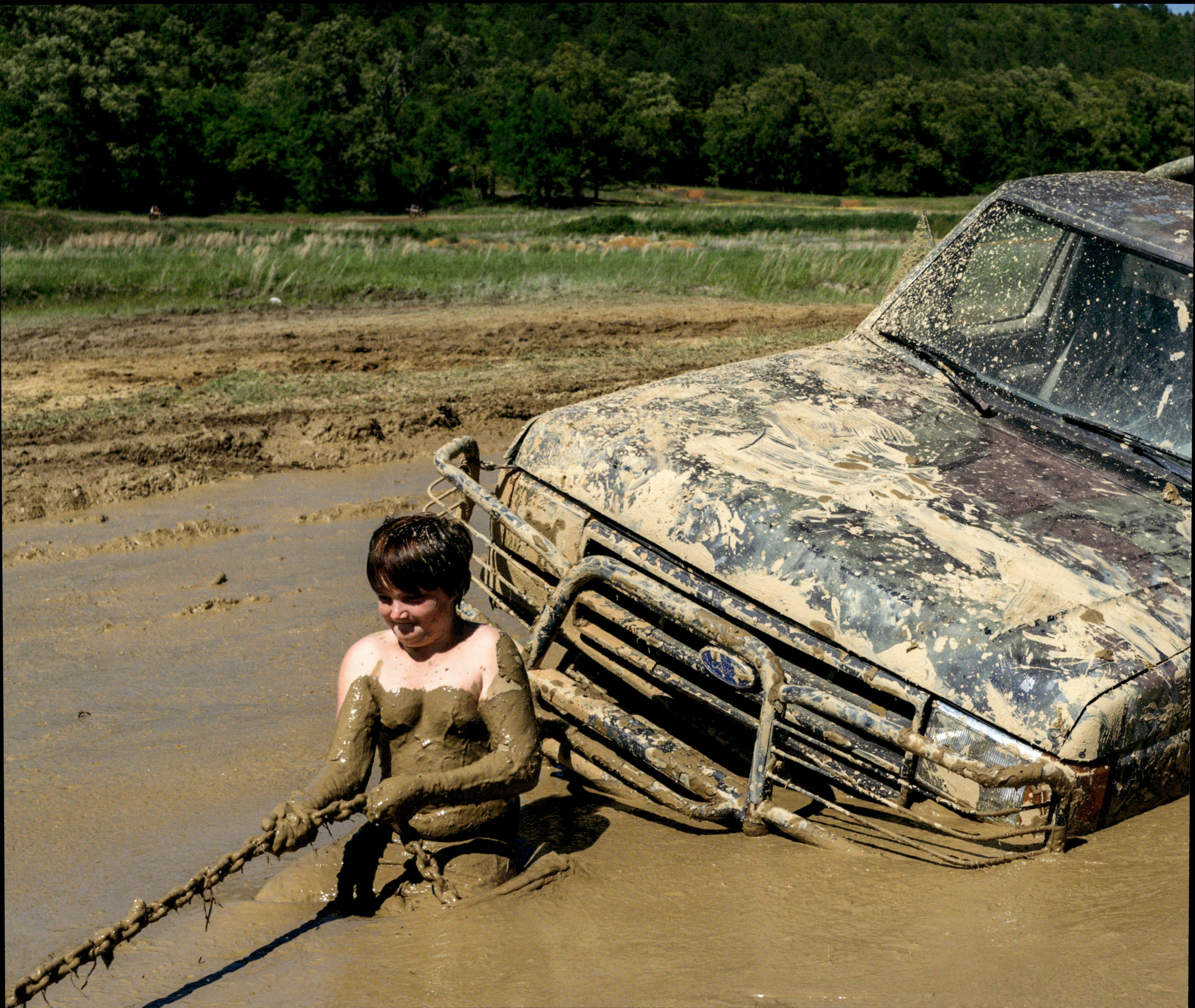

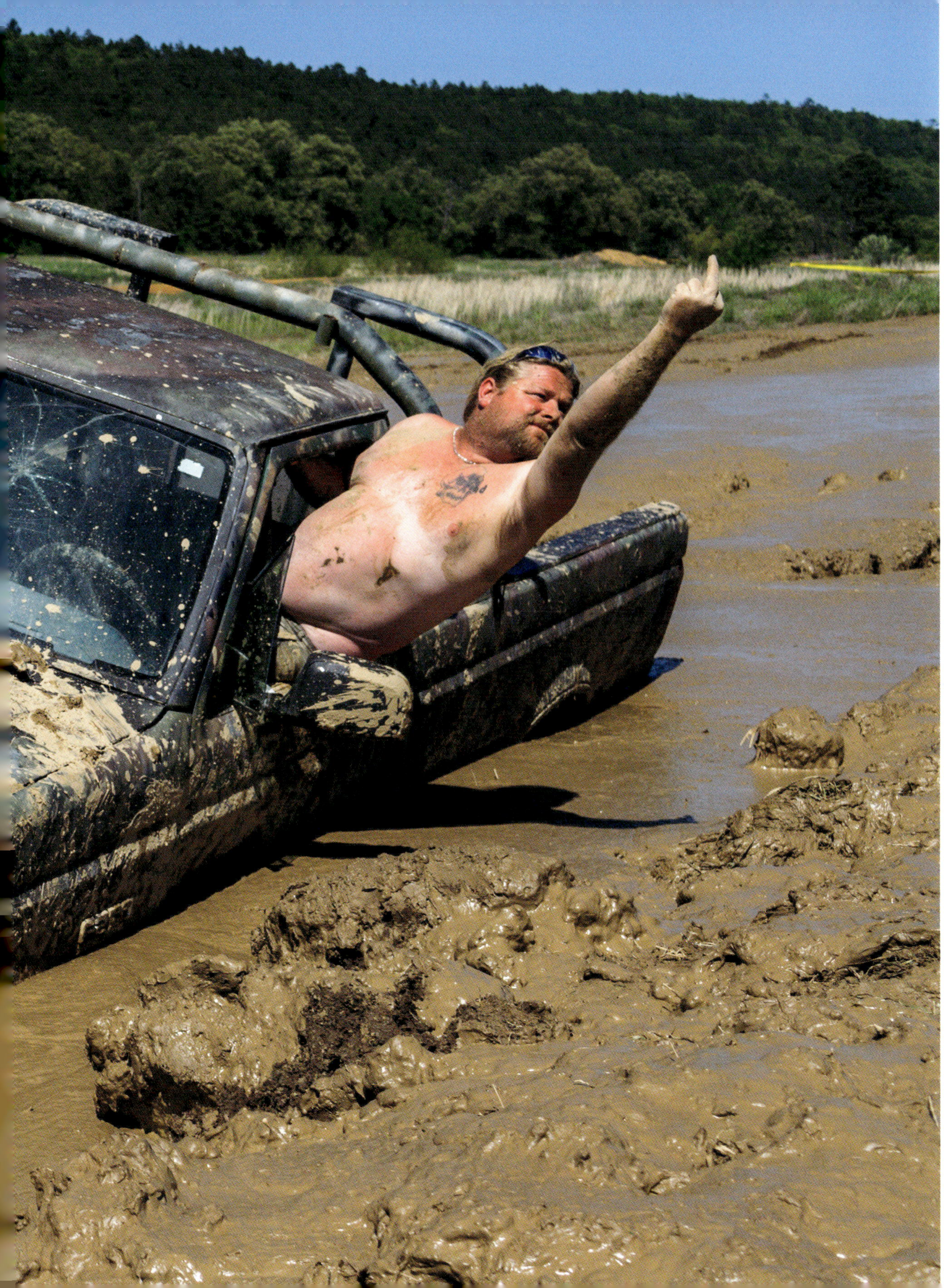

Mudding

Booneville, Arkansas, USA

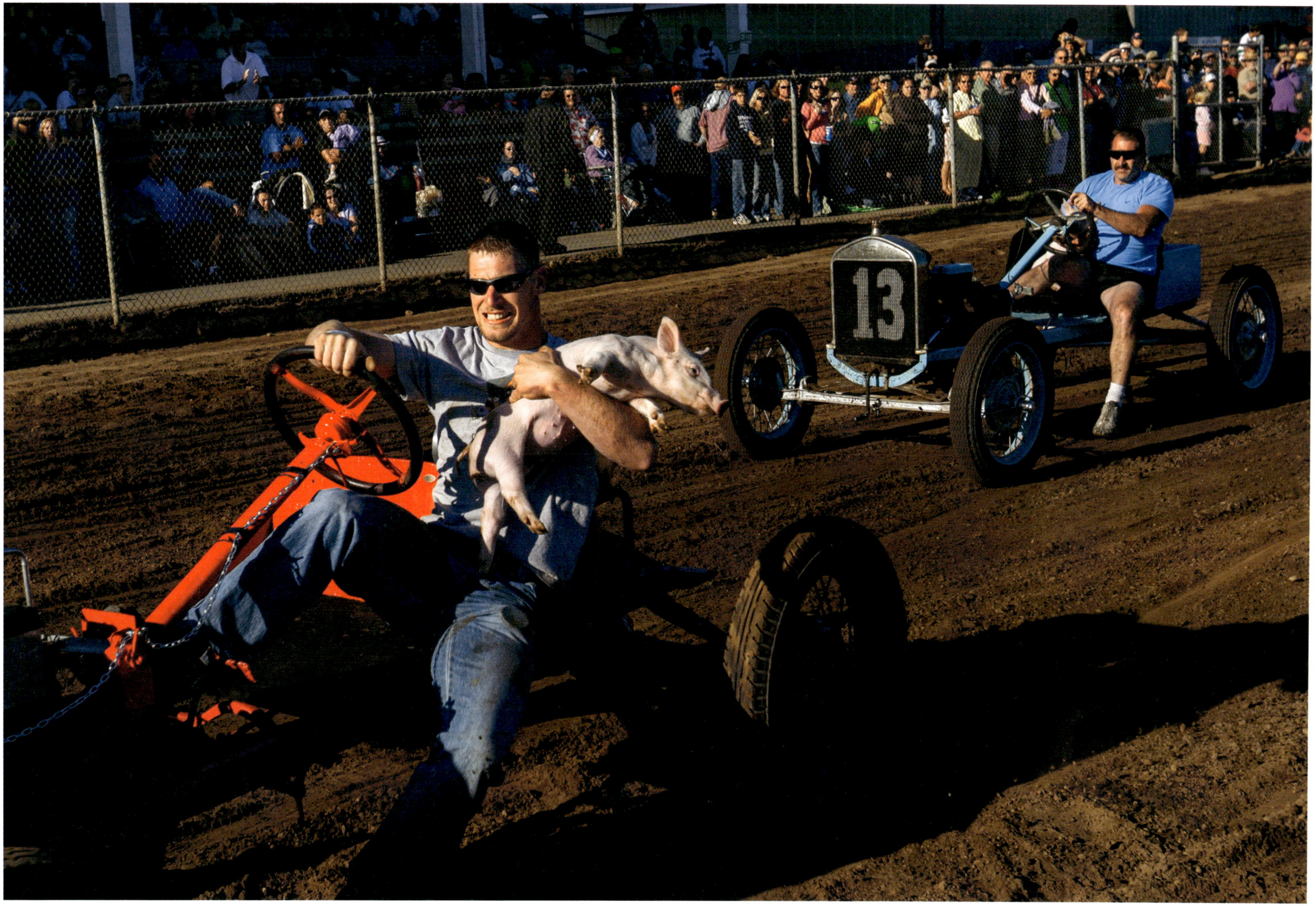

Pig-N-Ford Races

Tillamook, Oregon, USA

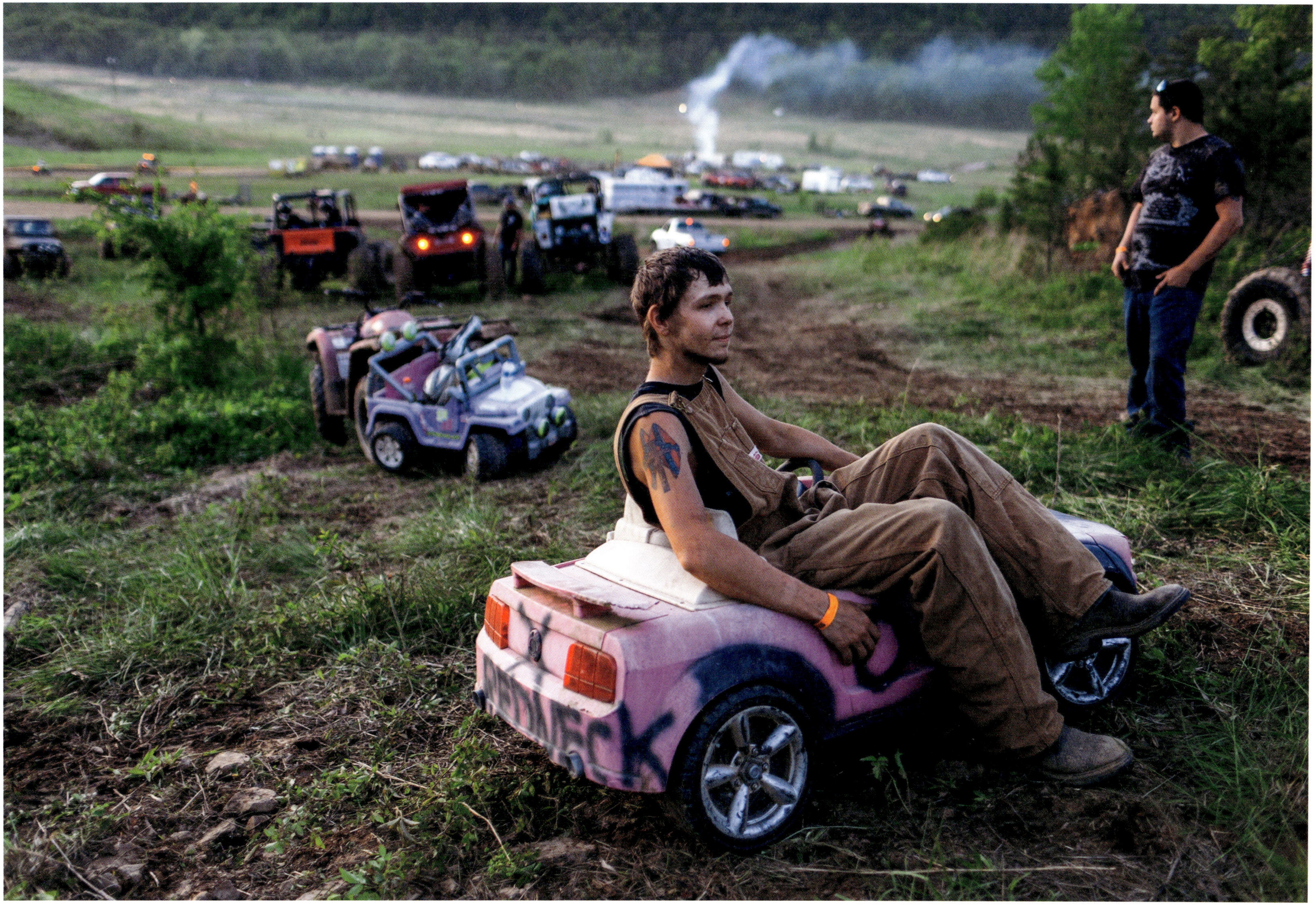

Extreme Barbie Jeep Racing

Booneville, Arkansas, USA

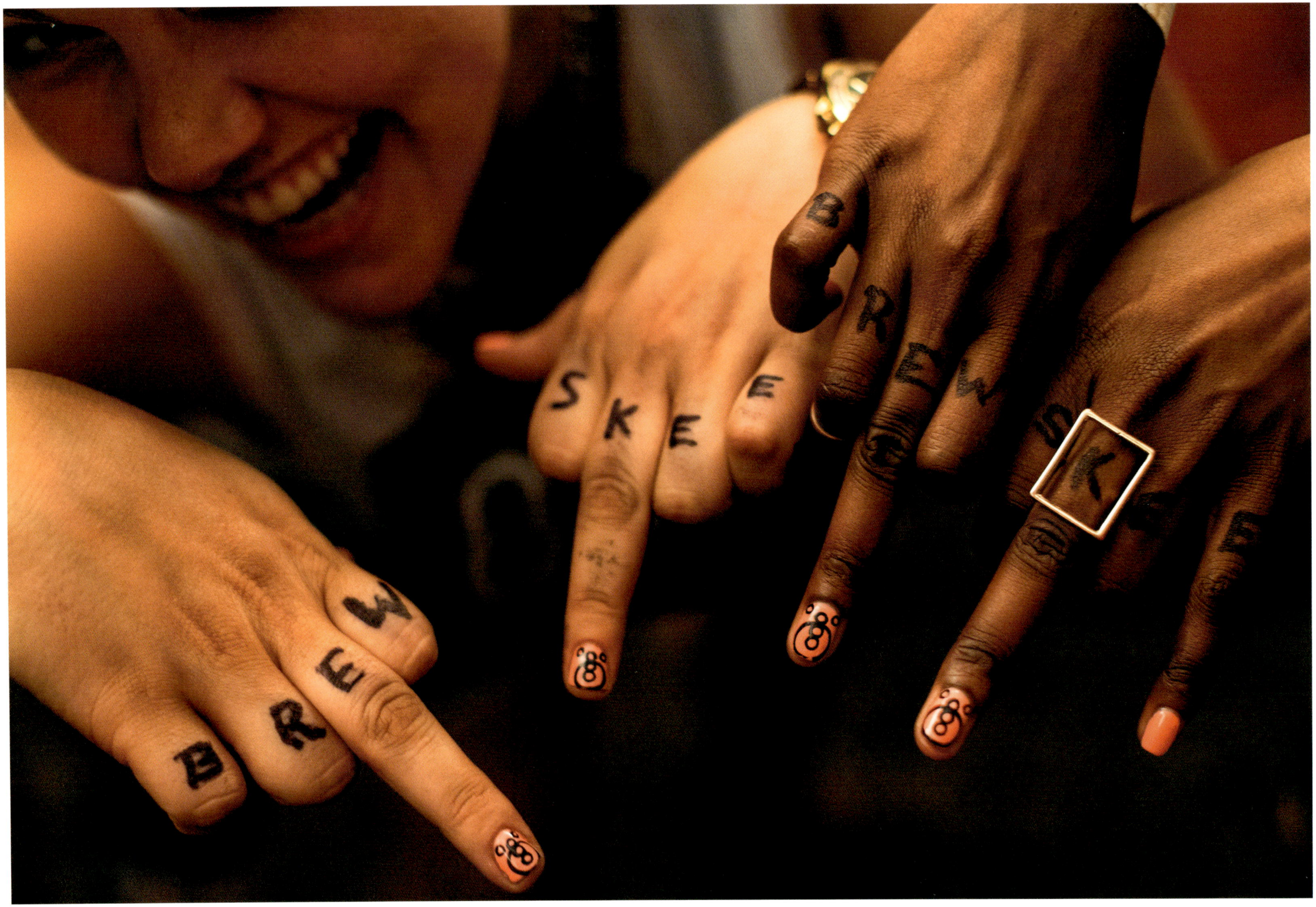

Brewskee-Ball® National Championships

Austin, Texas, USA

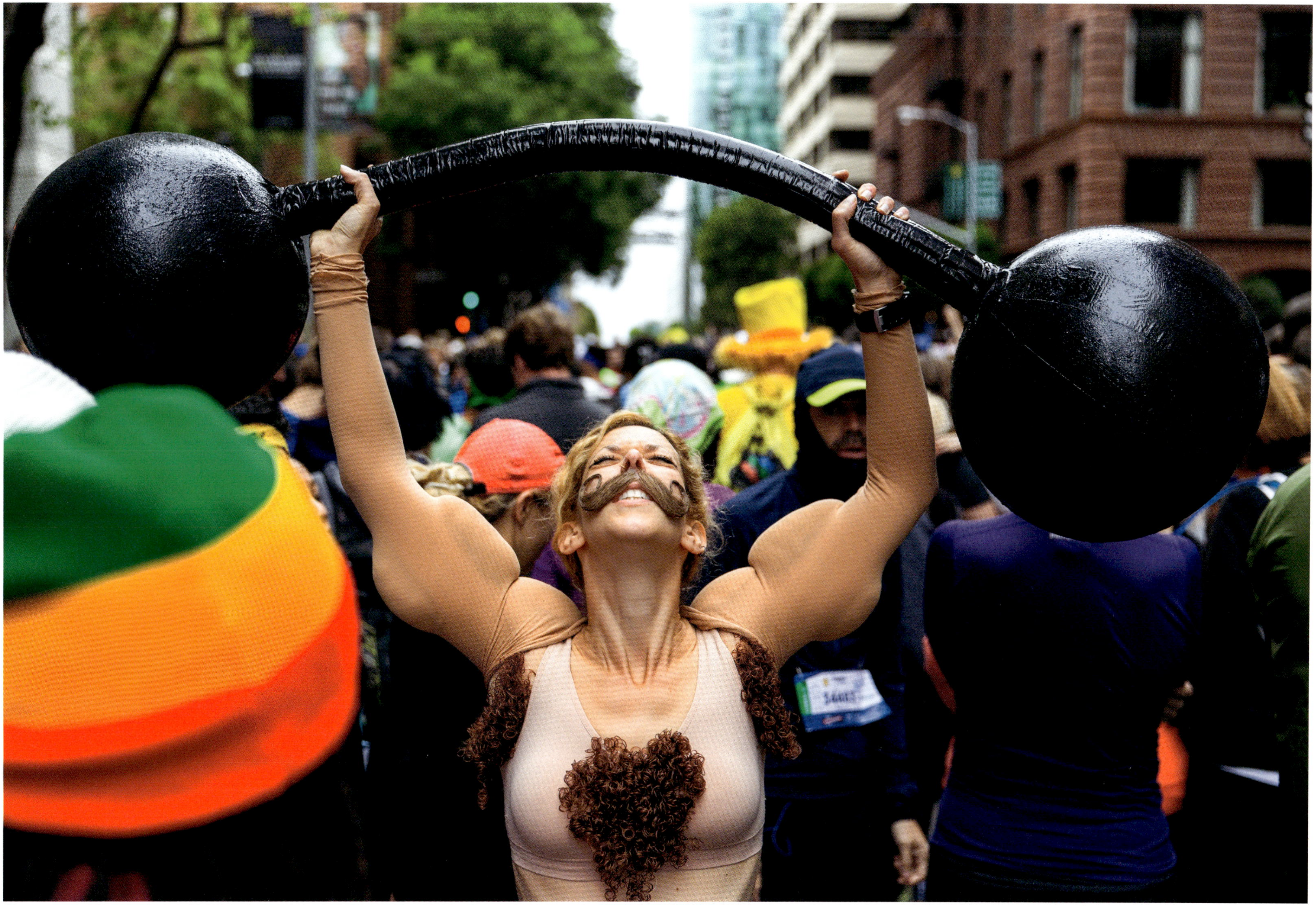

Bay to Breakers

San Francisco, California, USA

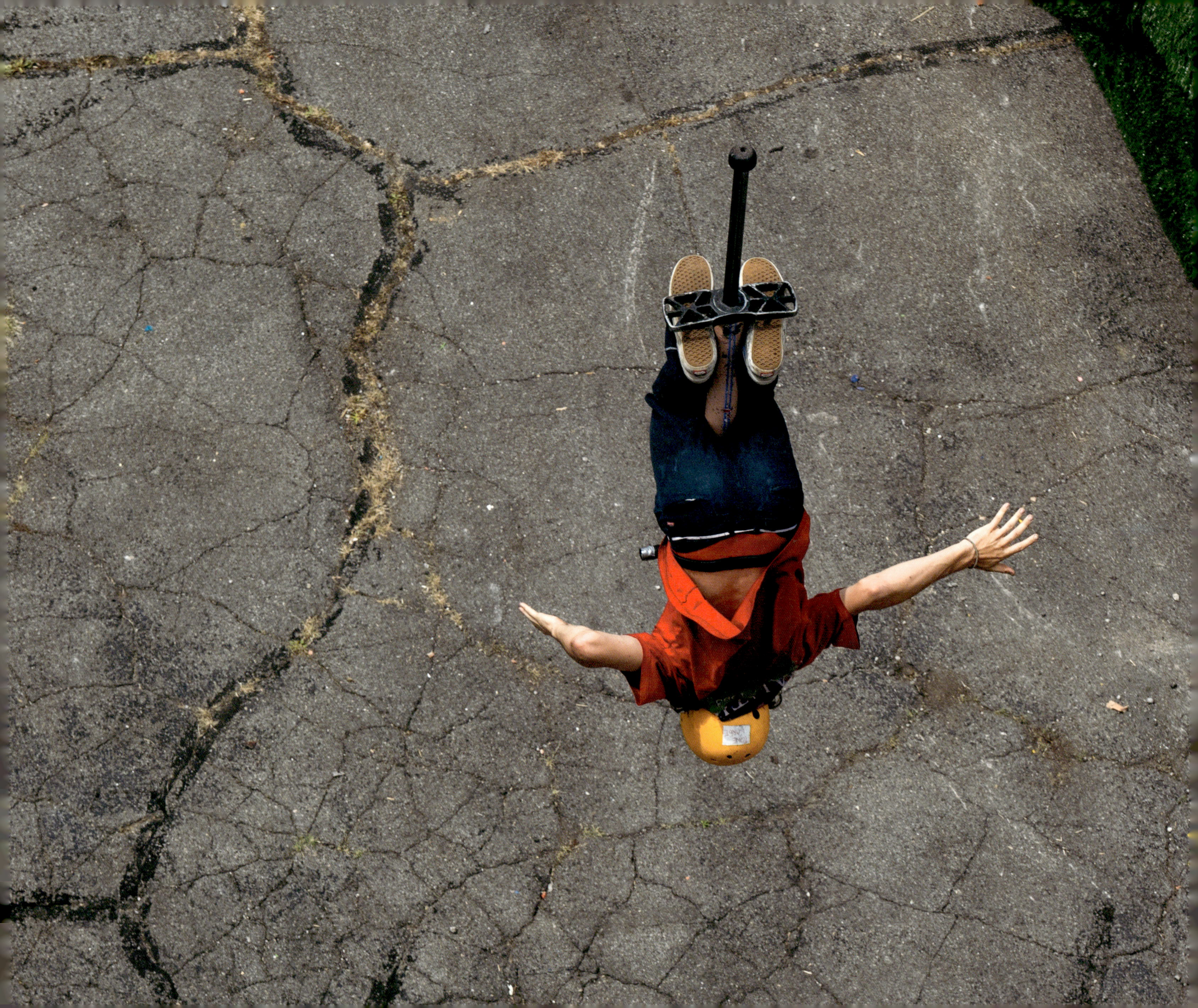

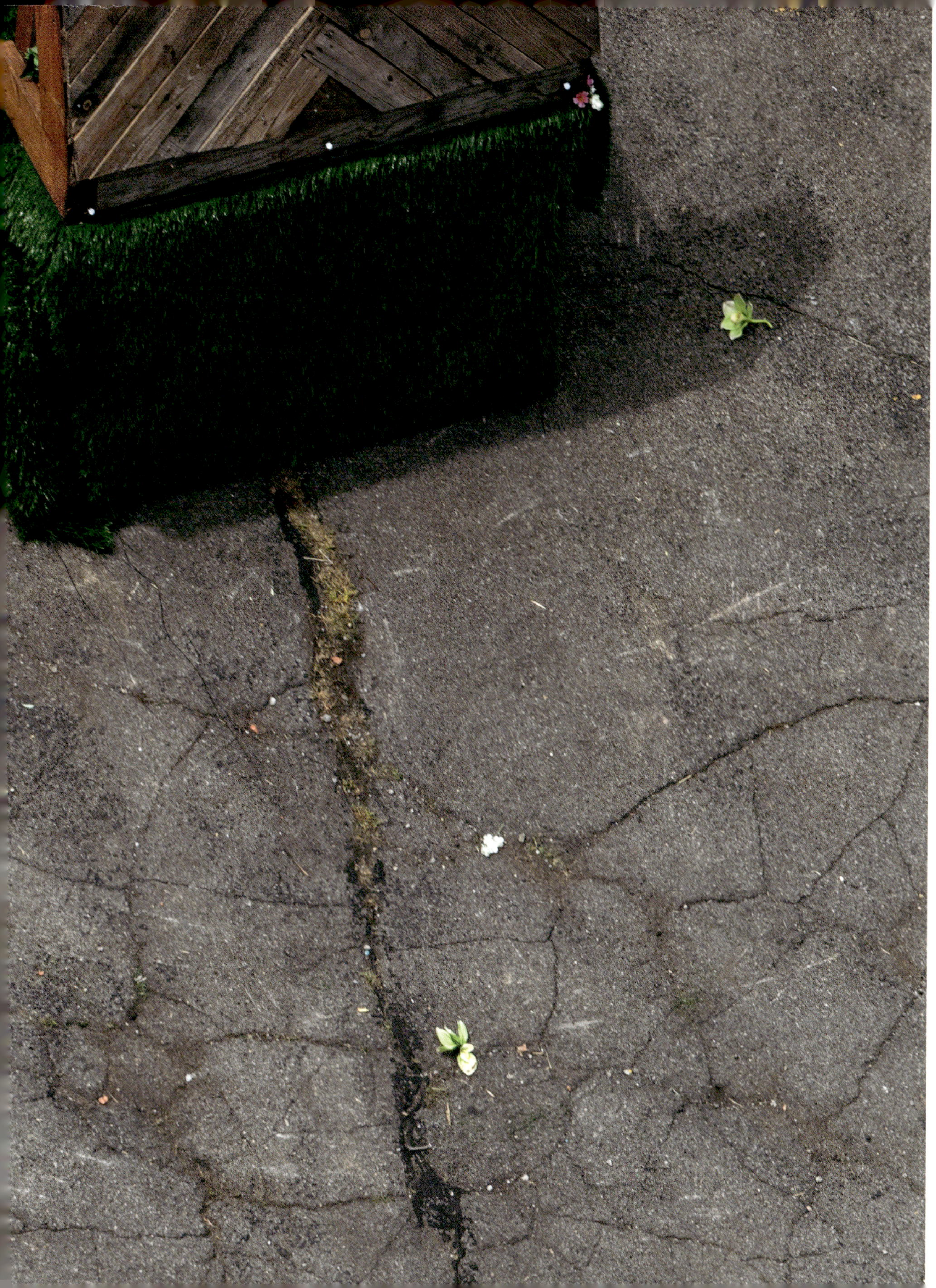

Pogopalooza

Pittsburgh, Pennsylvania, USA

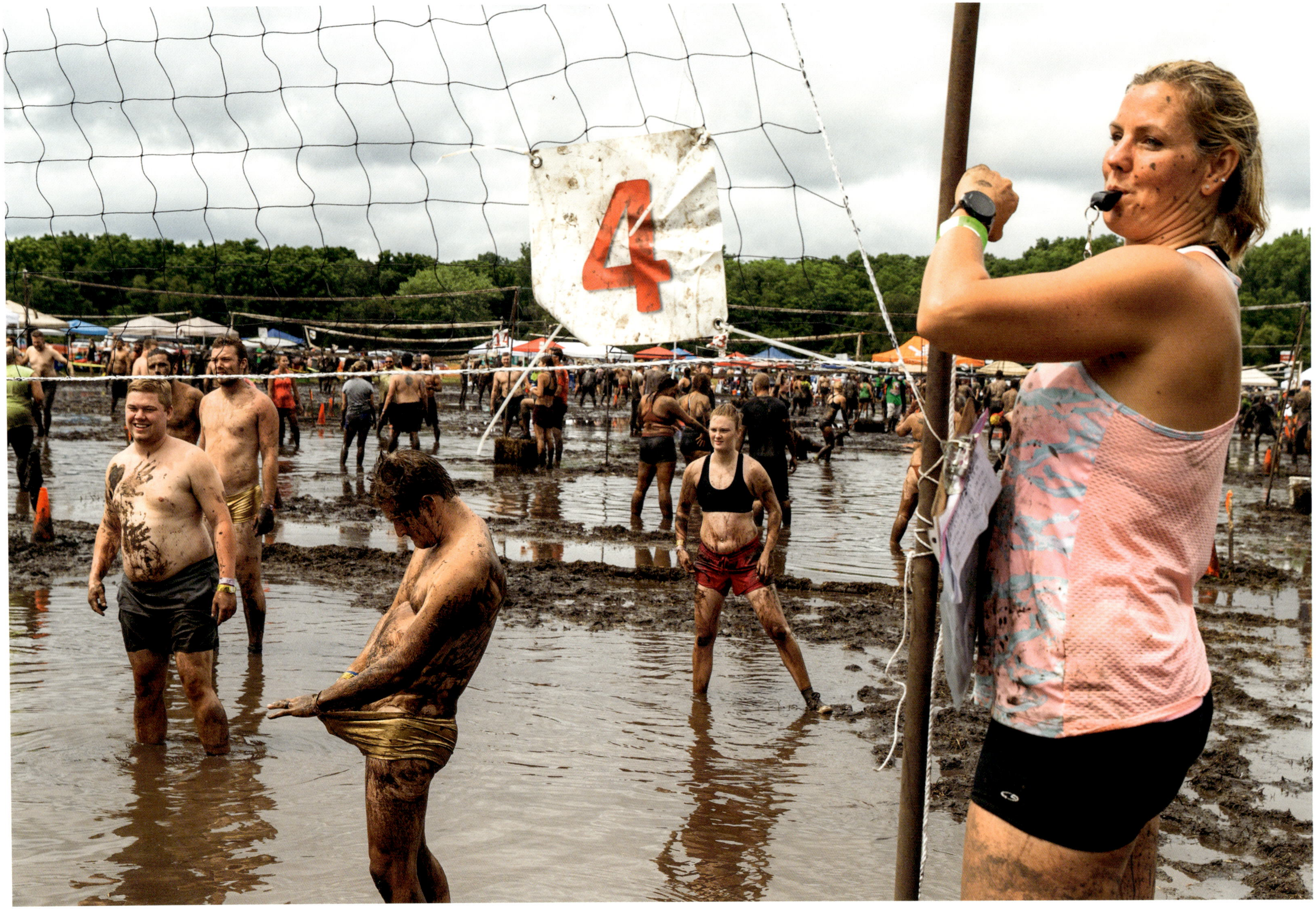

Mud Volleyball

Dayton, Ohio, USA

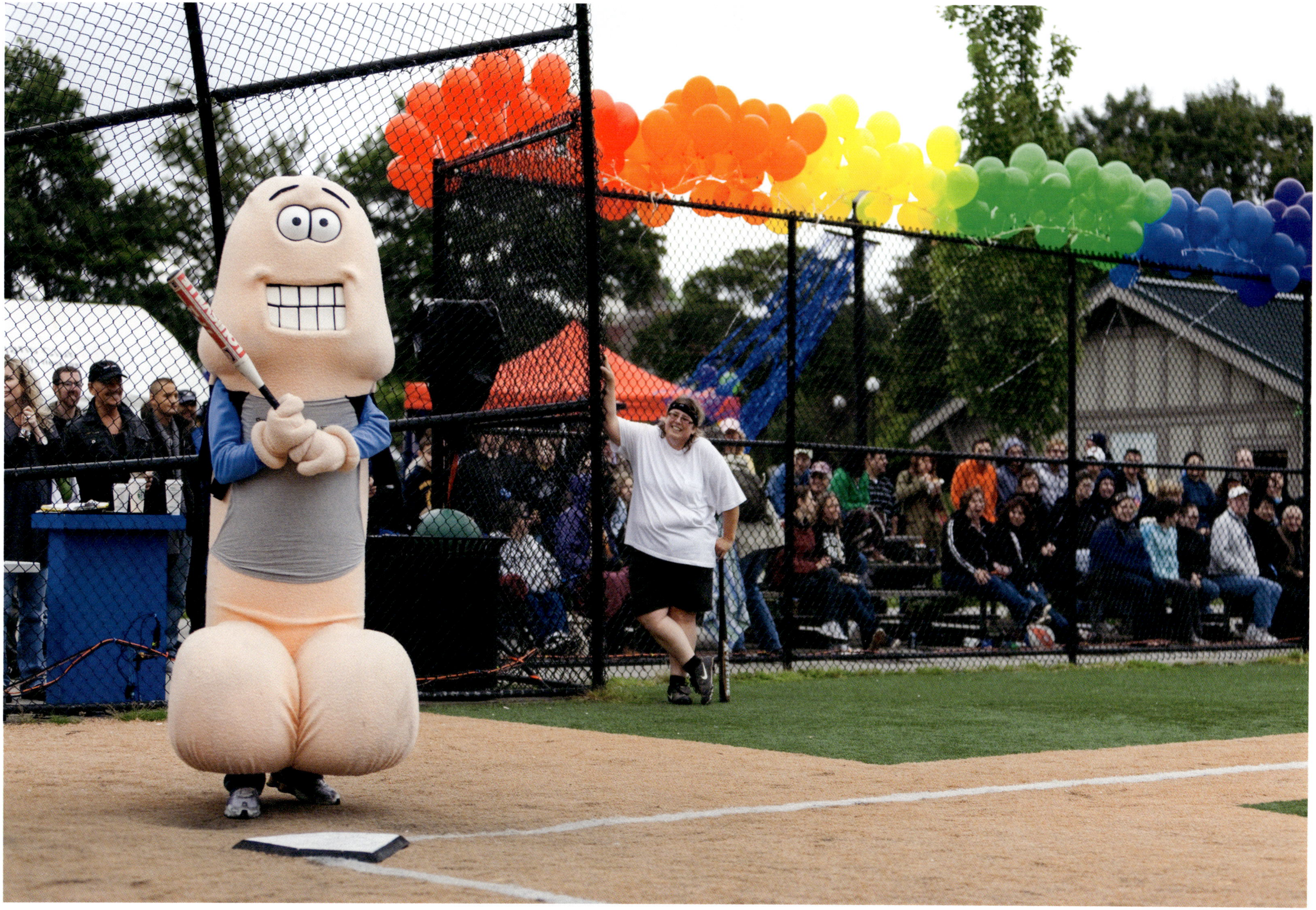

Drag Queen Softball

Seattle, Washington, USA

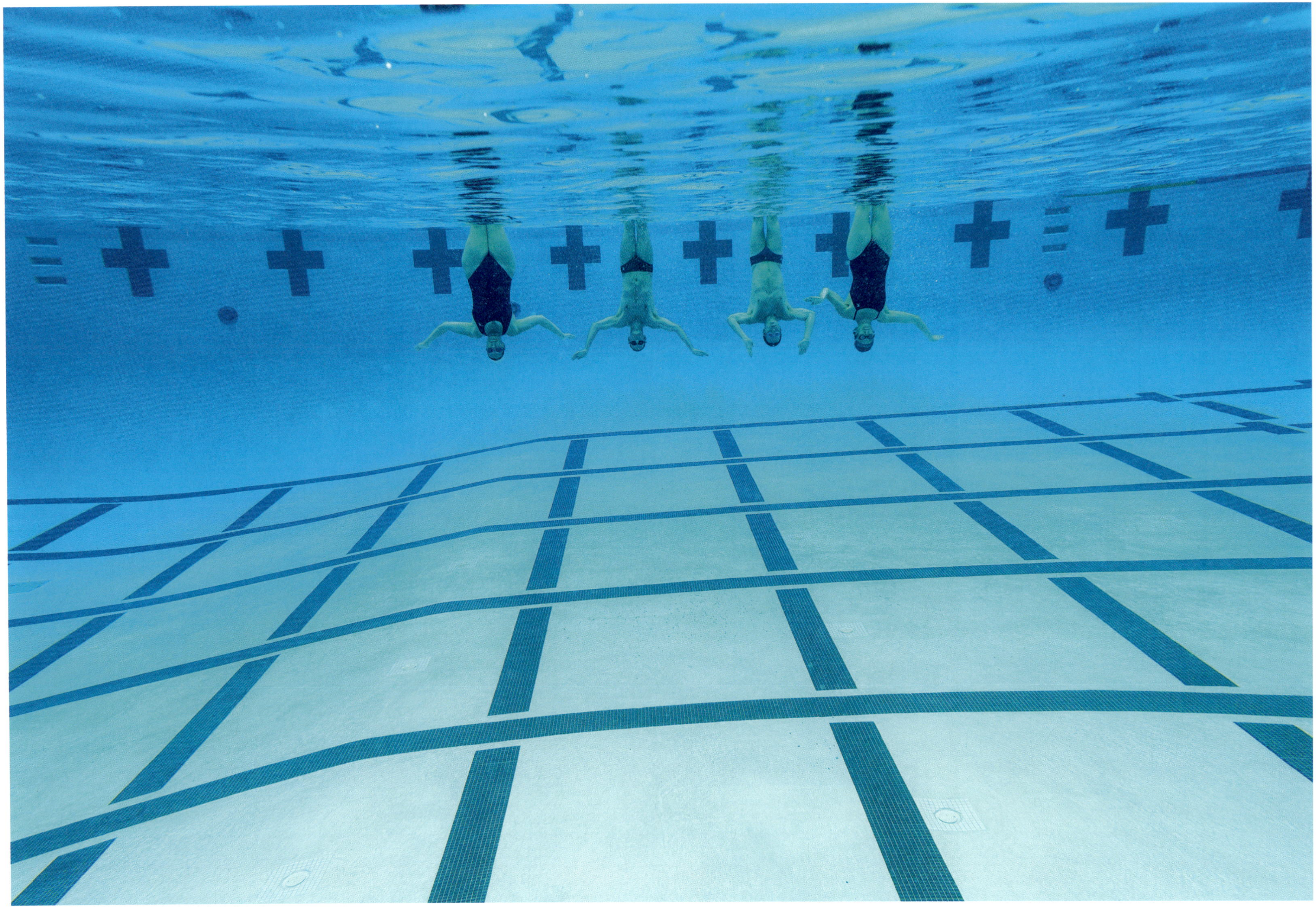

Co-Ed Synchronized Swimming

Berkeley, California, USA

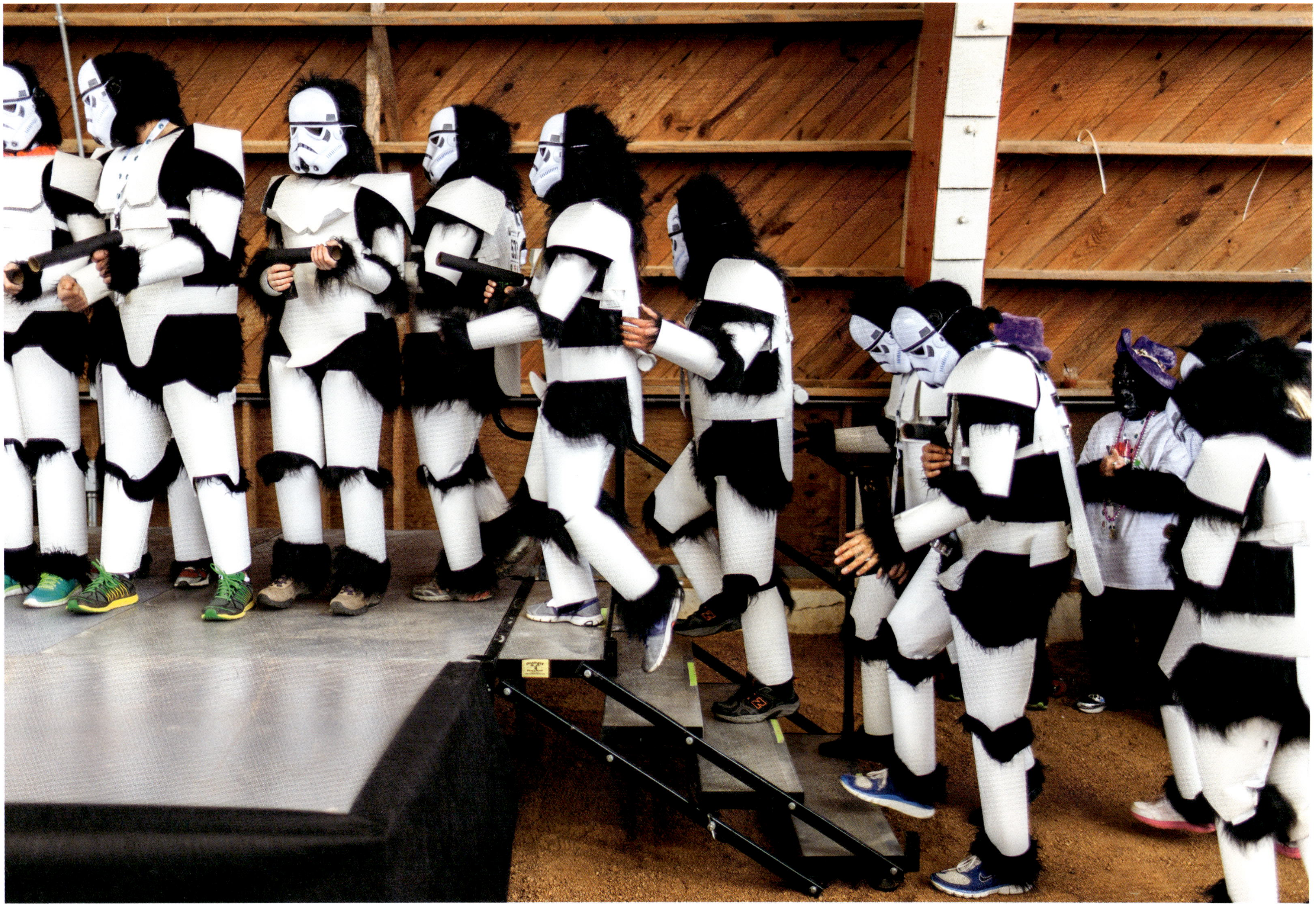

Gorilla Run

Austin, Texas, USA

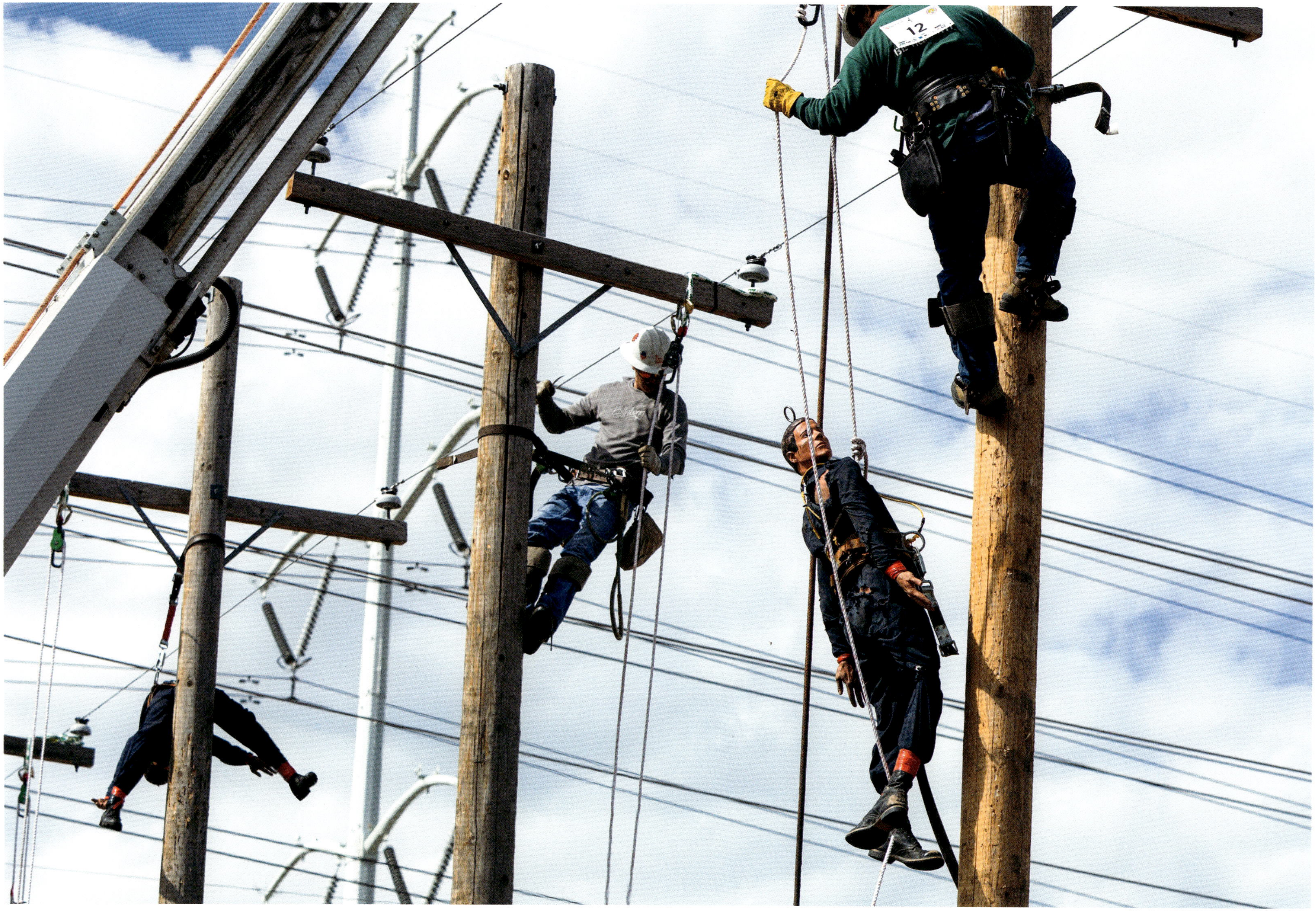

Lineman's Rodeo

West Valley City, Utah, USA

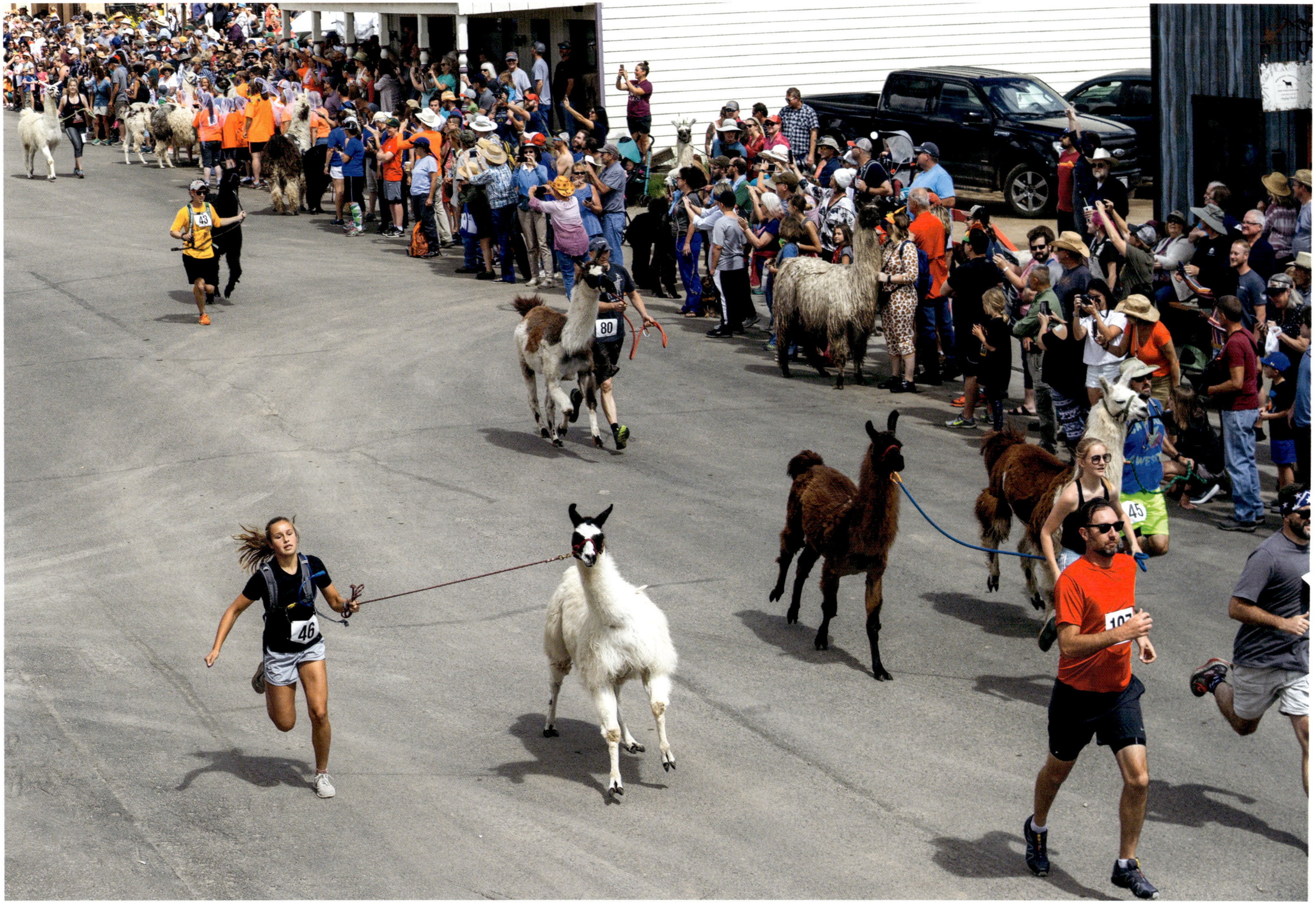

Llama Rama Race

Fairplay, Colorado, USA

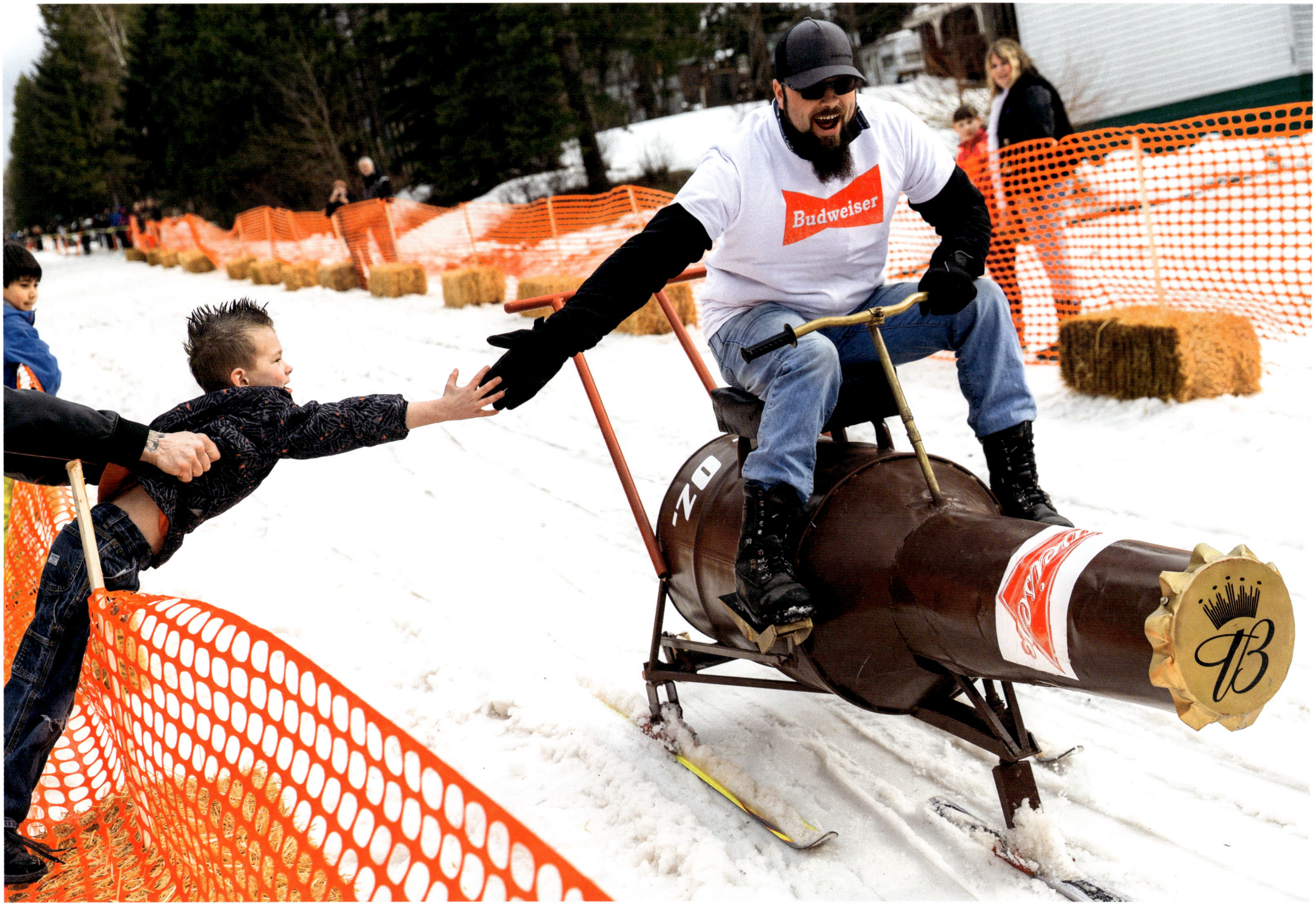

Barstool Ski Racing

Martin City, Montana, USA

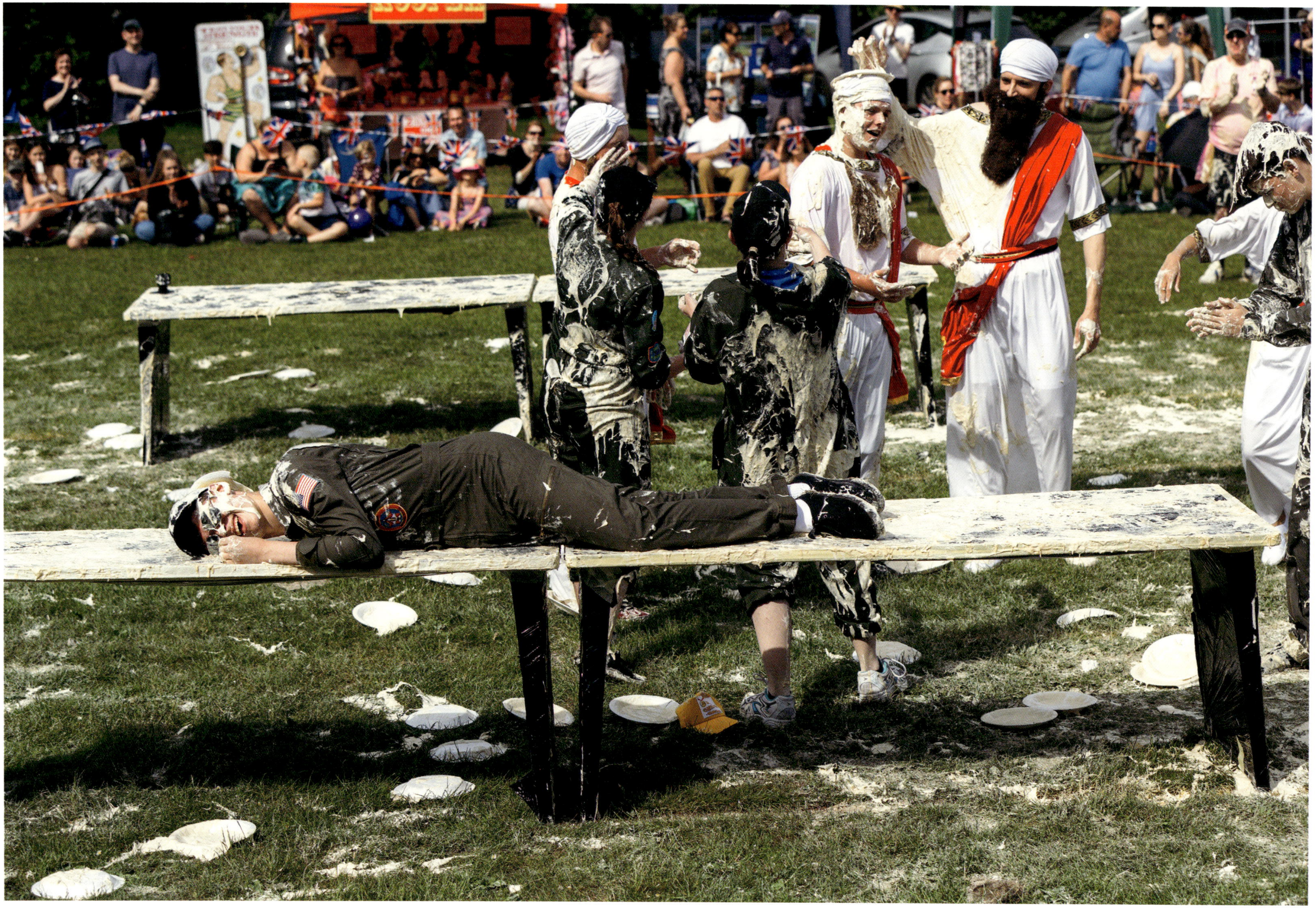

World Custard Pie Championship

Maidstone, England, UK

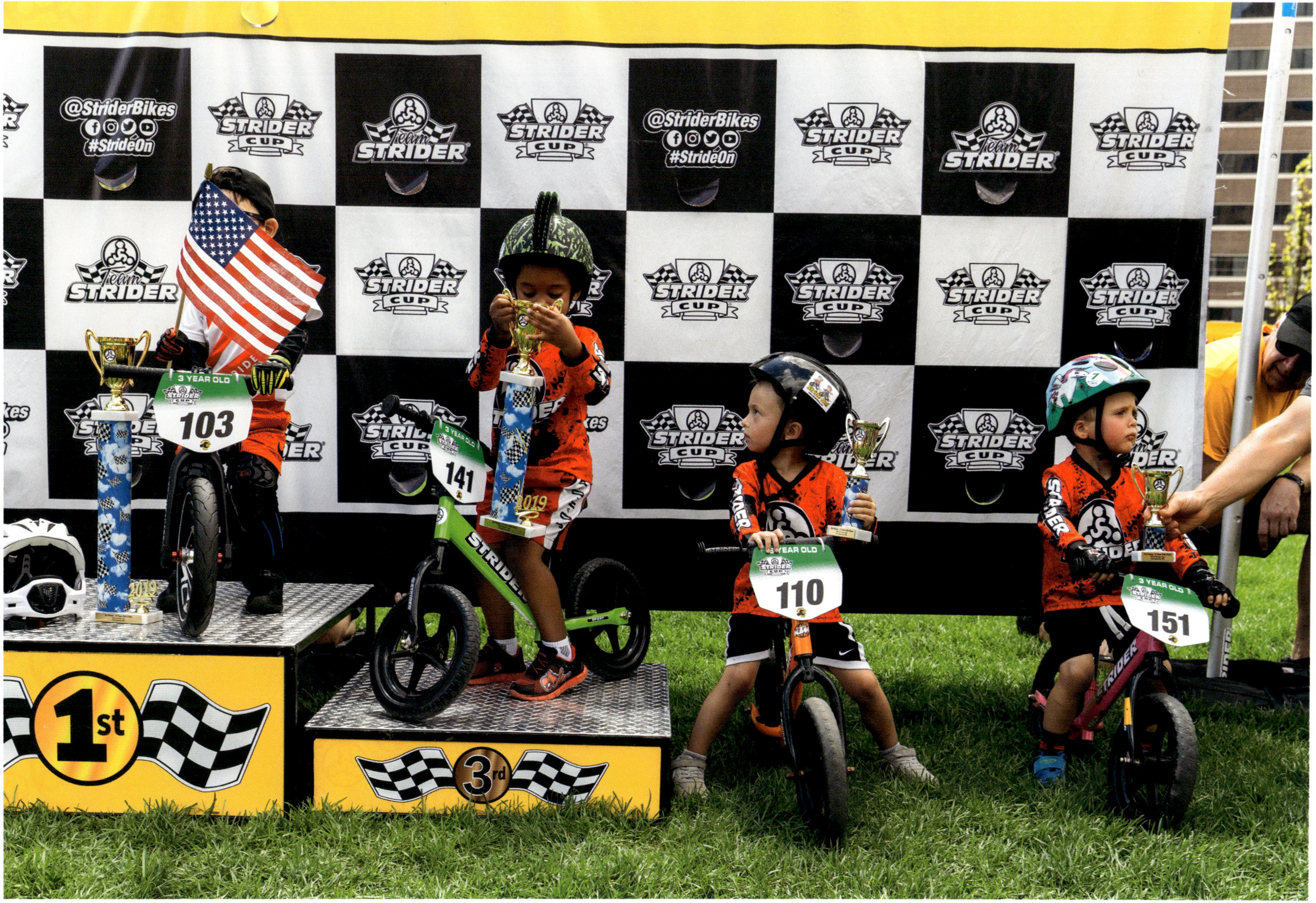

Strider Cup®
Minneapolis, Minnesota, USA

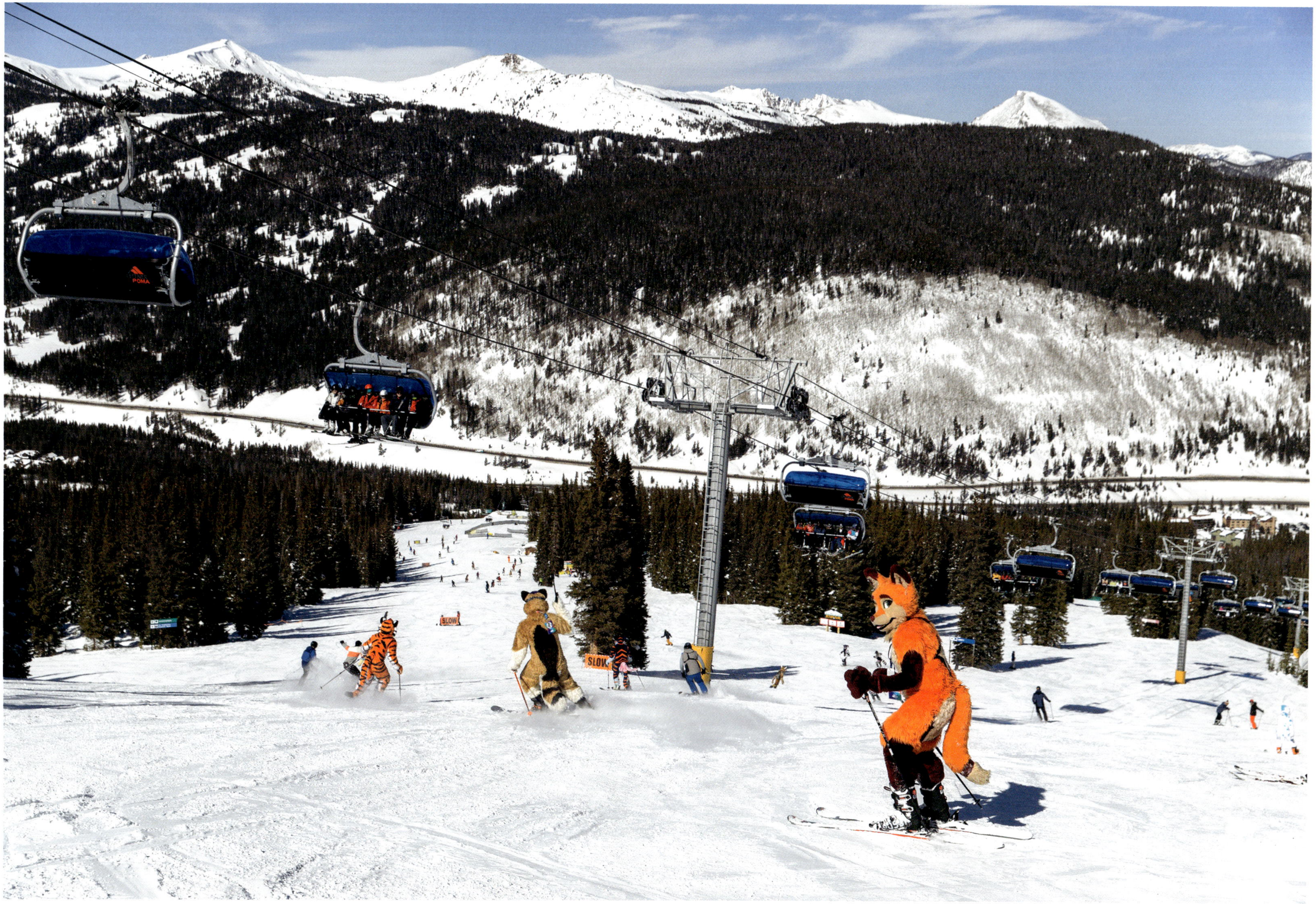

Furry Ski Weekend

Copper Mountain, Colorado, USA

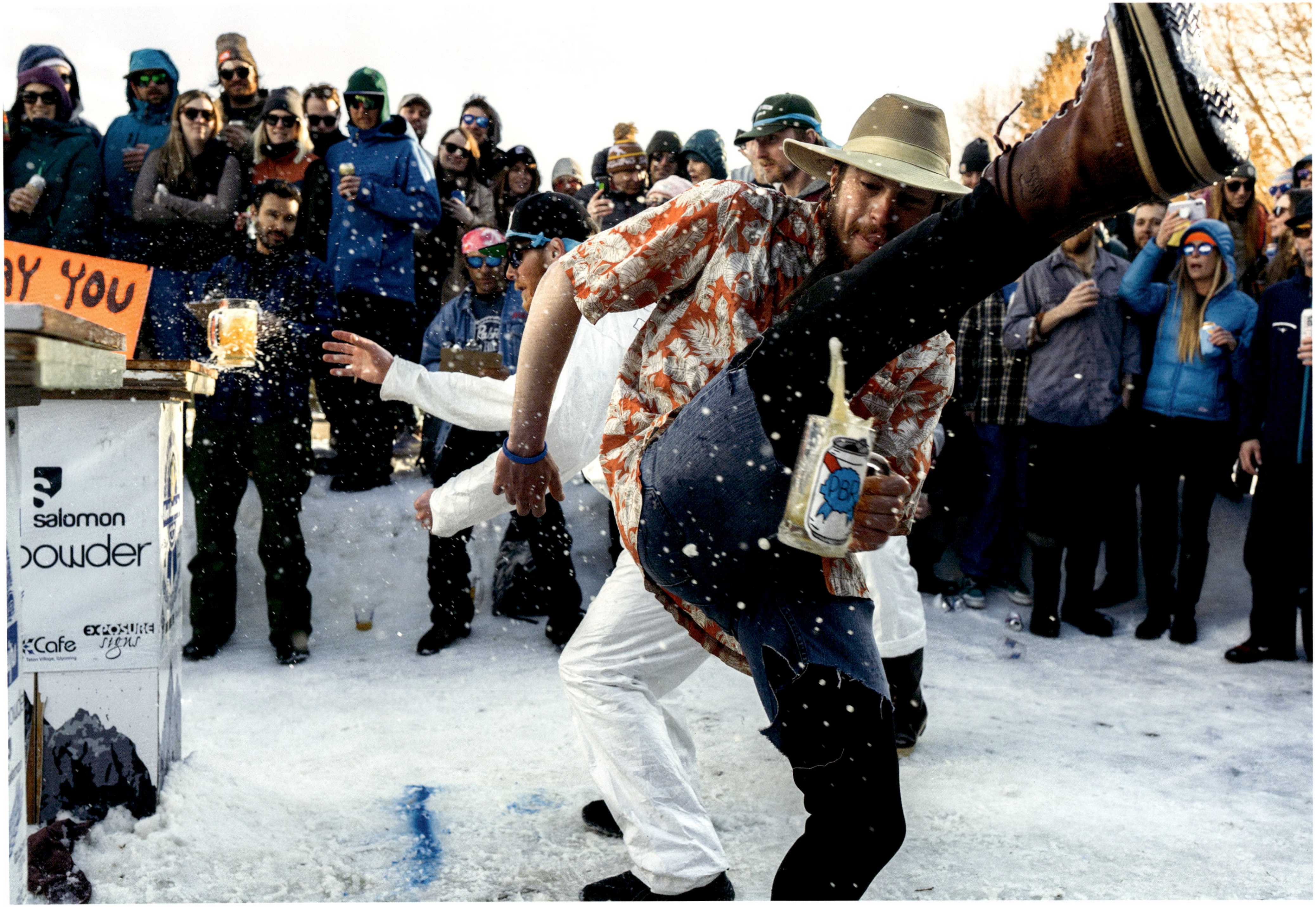

Gelände Quaffing World Championships

Teton Village, Wyoming, USA

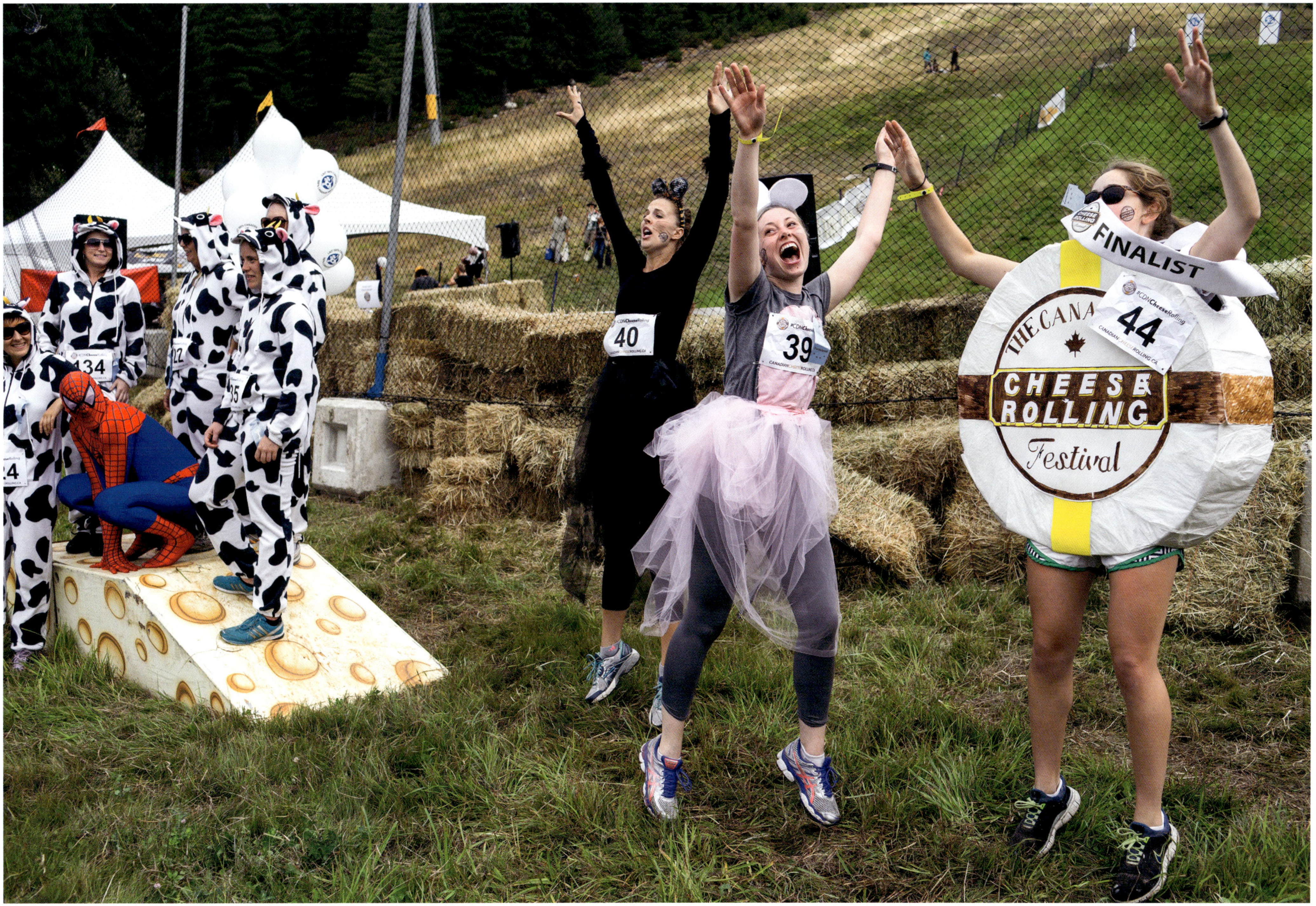

Canadian Cheese Rolling

Whistler, British Columbia, Canada

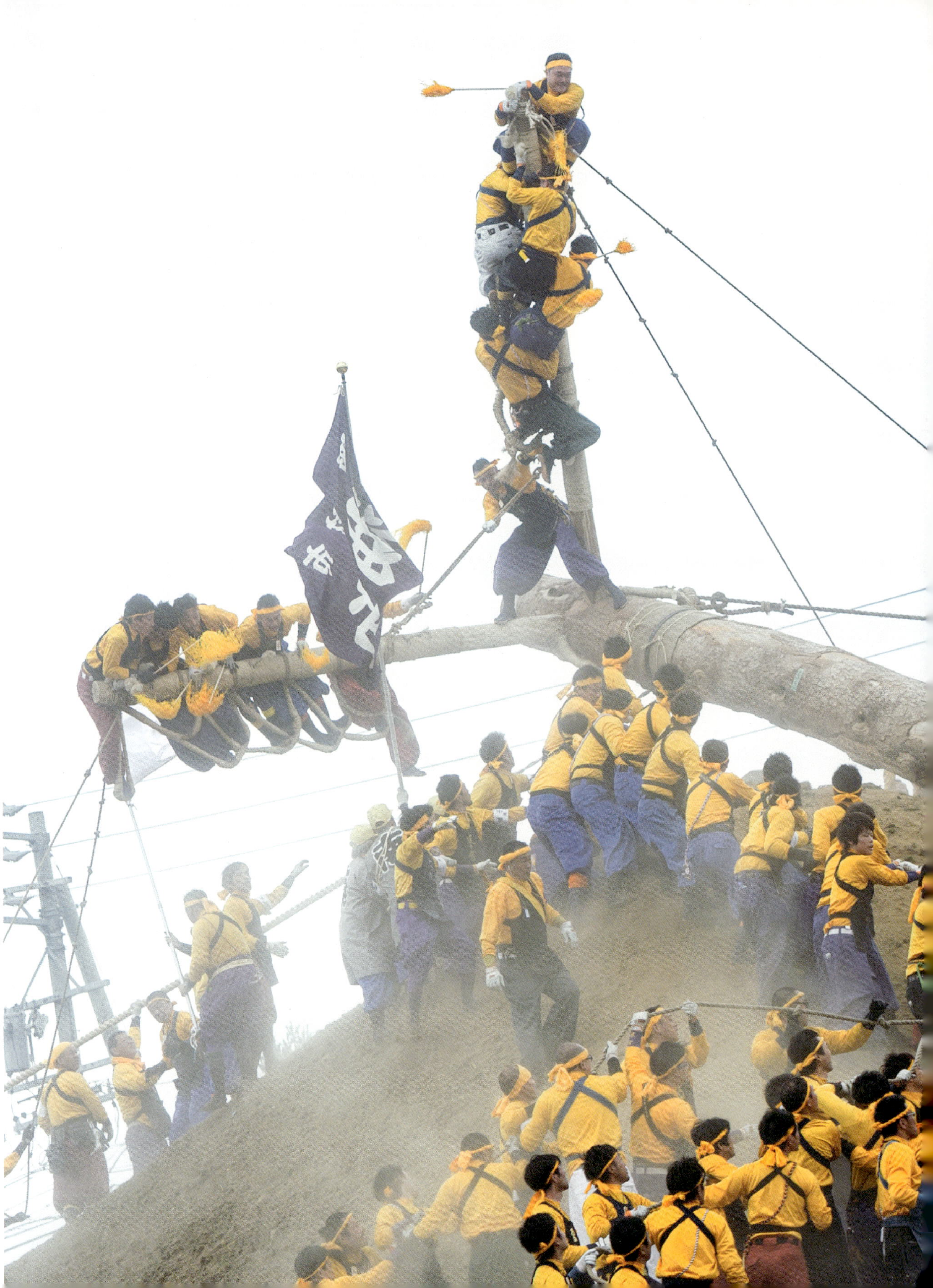

Log Riding

Chino, Japan

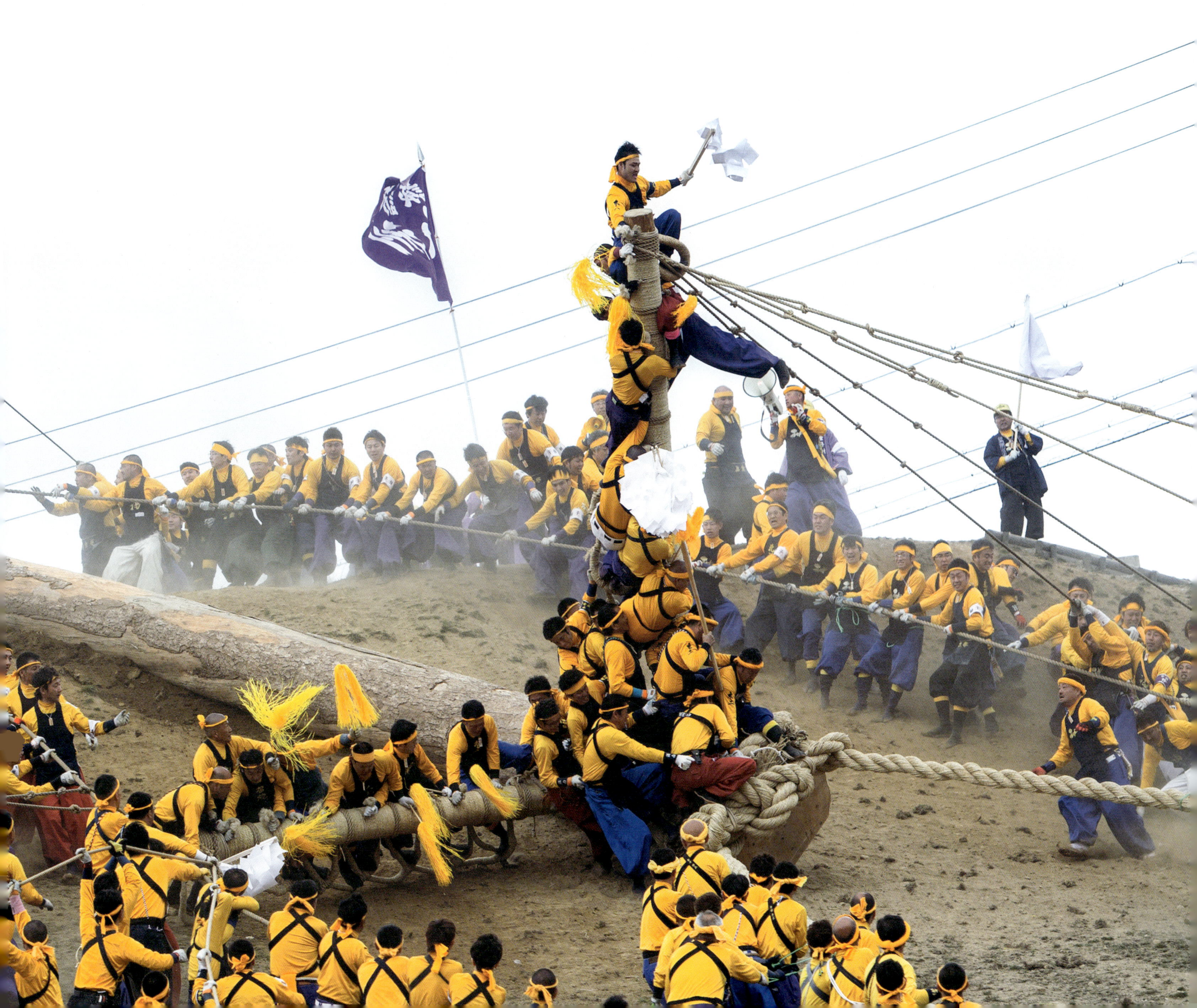

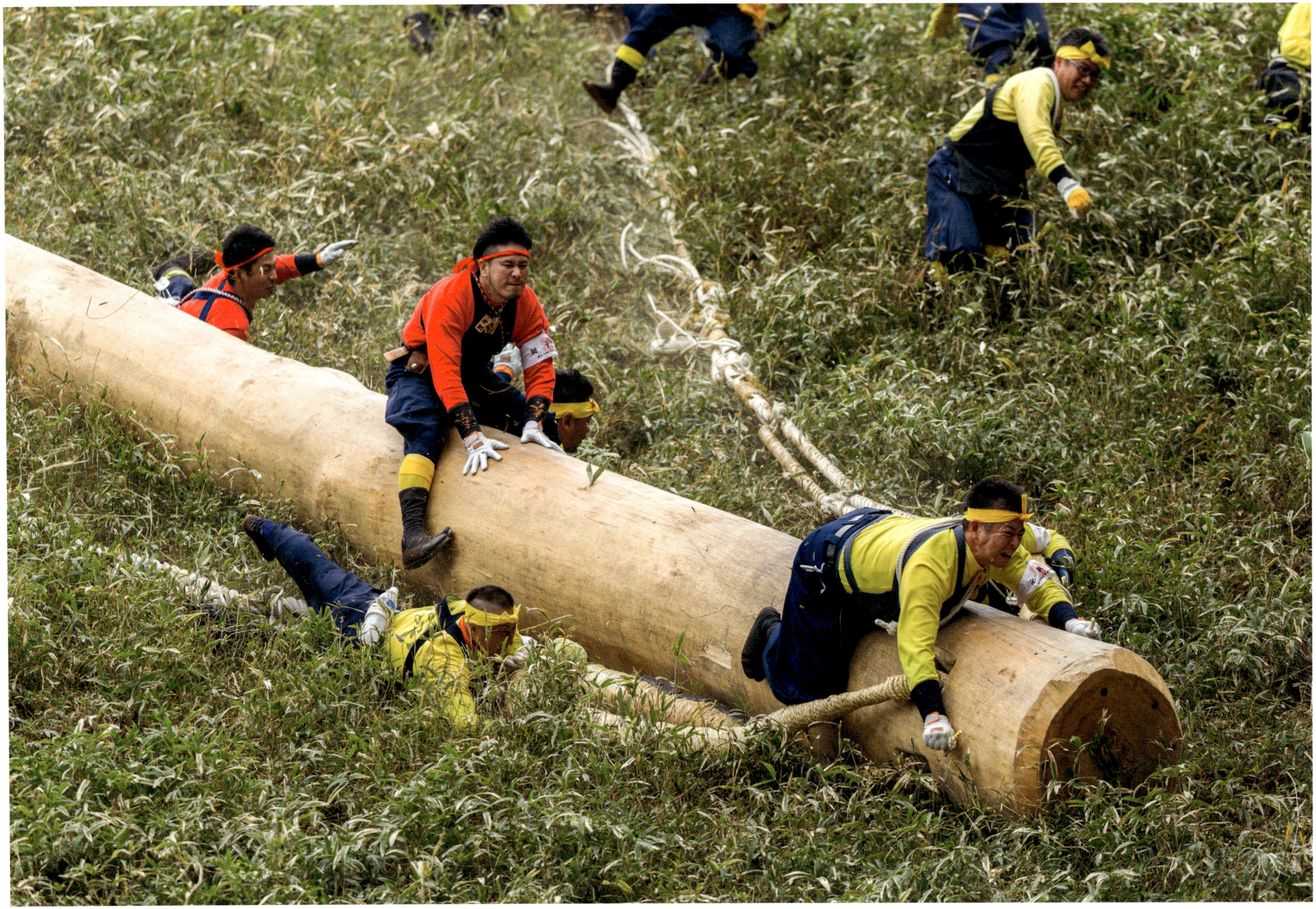

Log Riding

Suwa, Japan

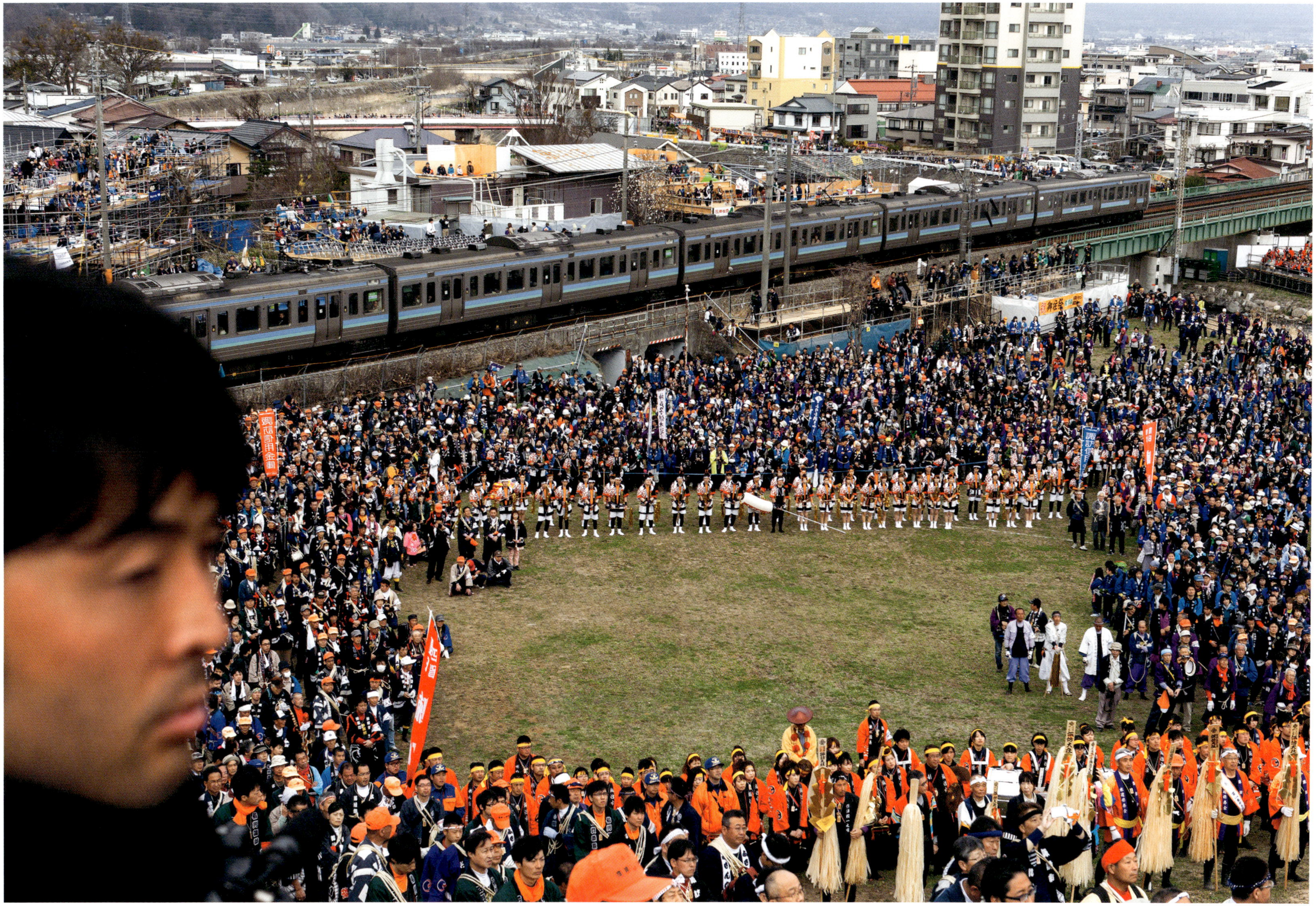

Log Riding

Chino, Japan

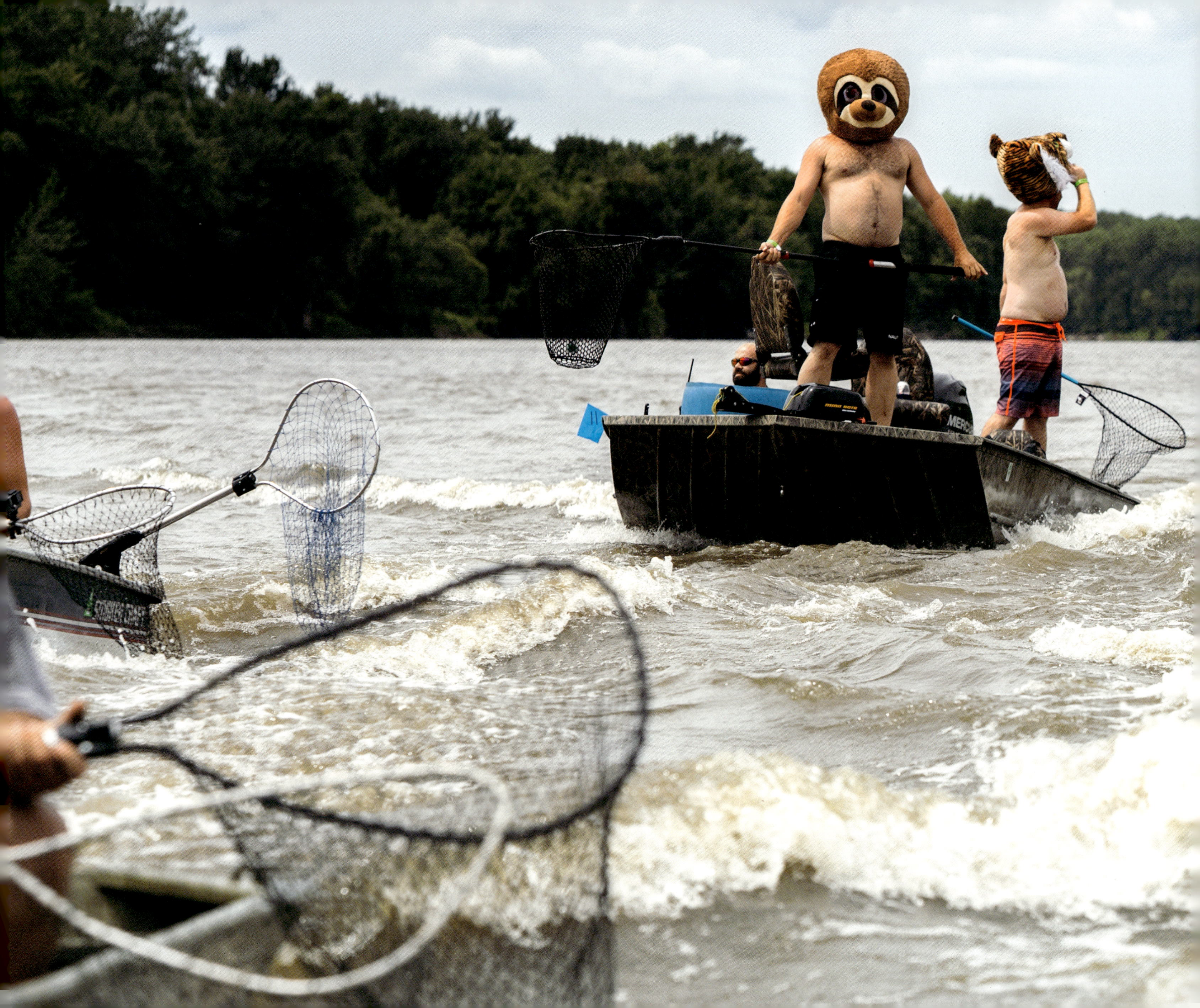

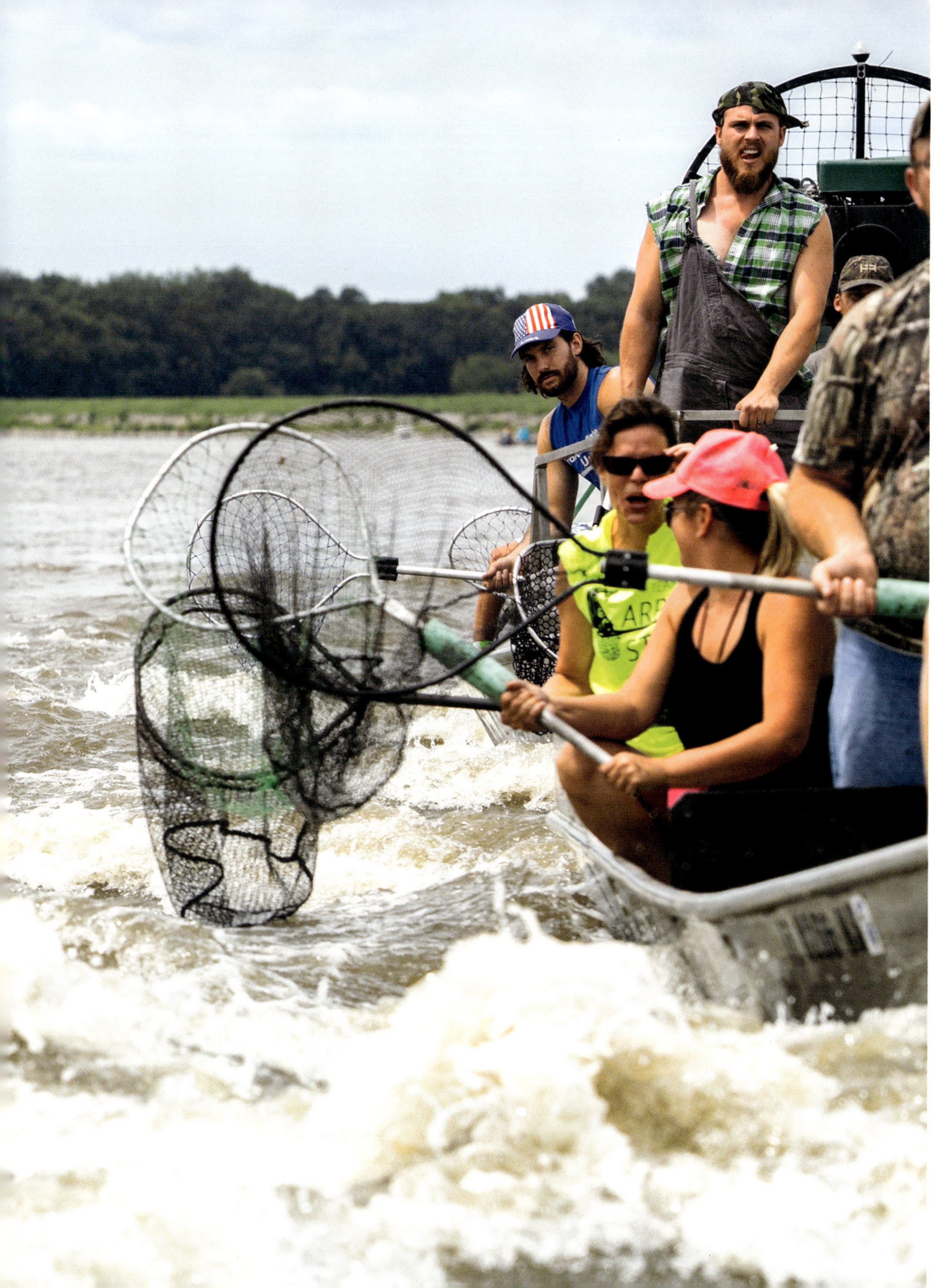

Redneck Fishing

Bath, Illinois, USA

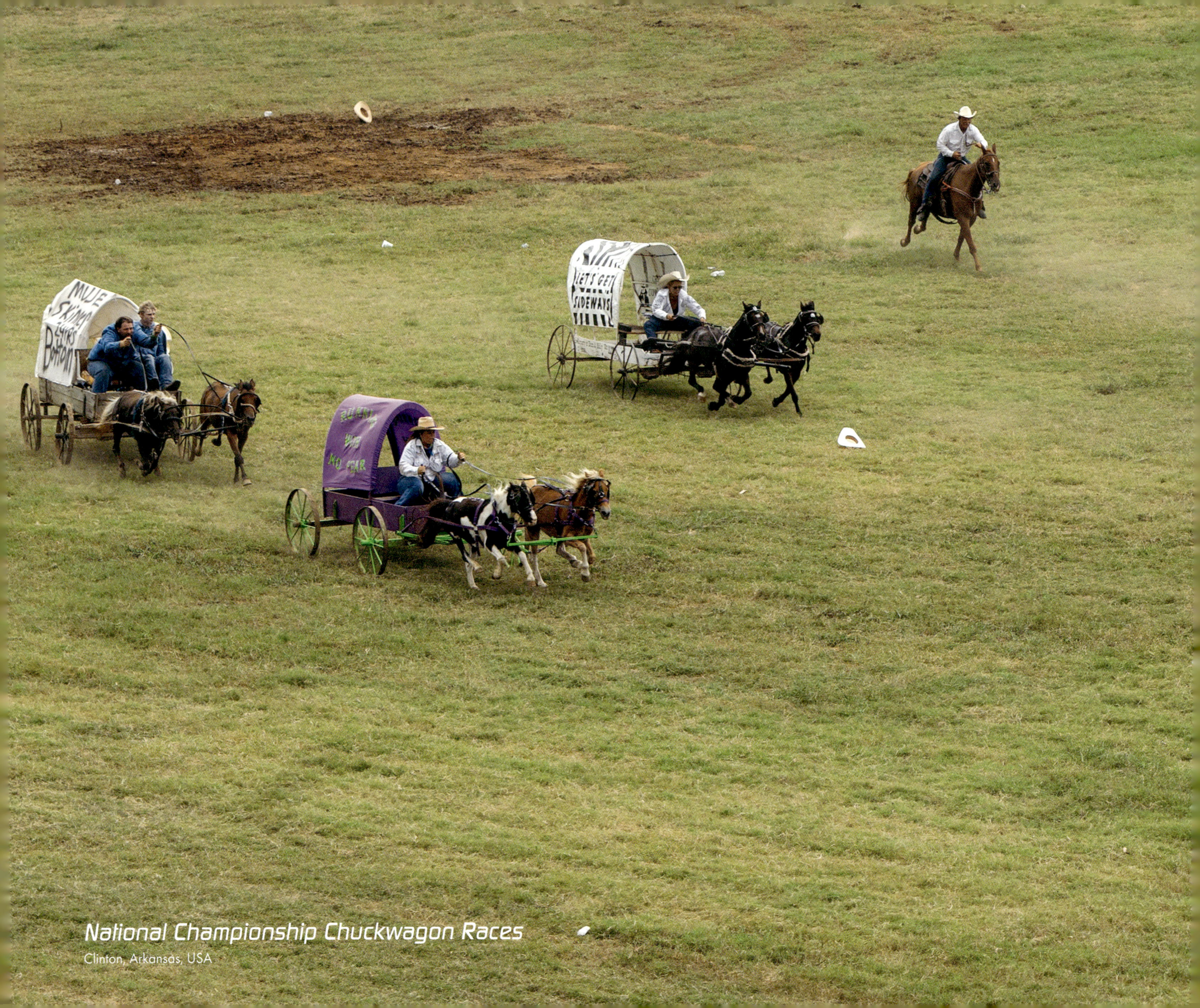

National Championship Chuckwagon Races

Clinton, Arkansas, USA

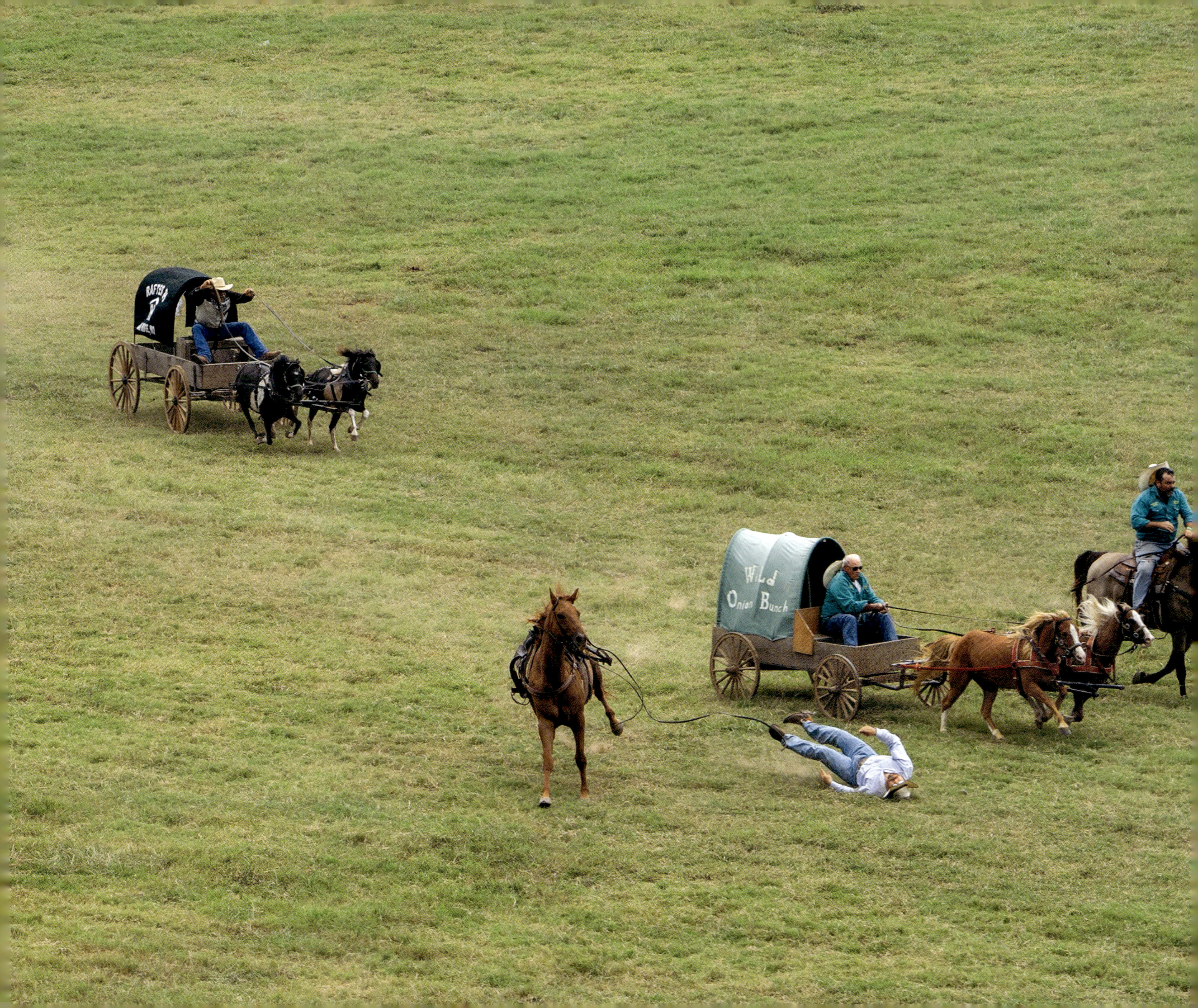
Wild
Onion Bunch

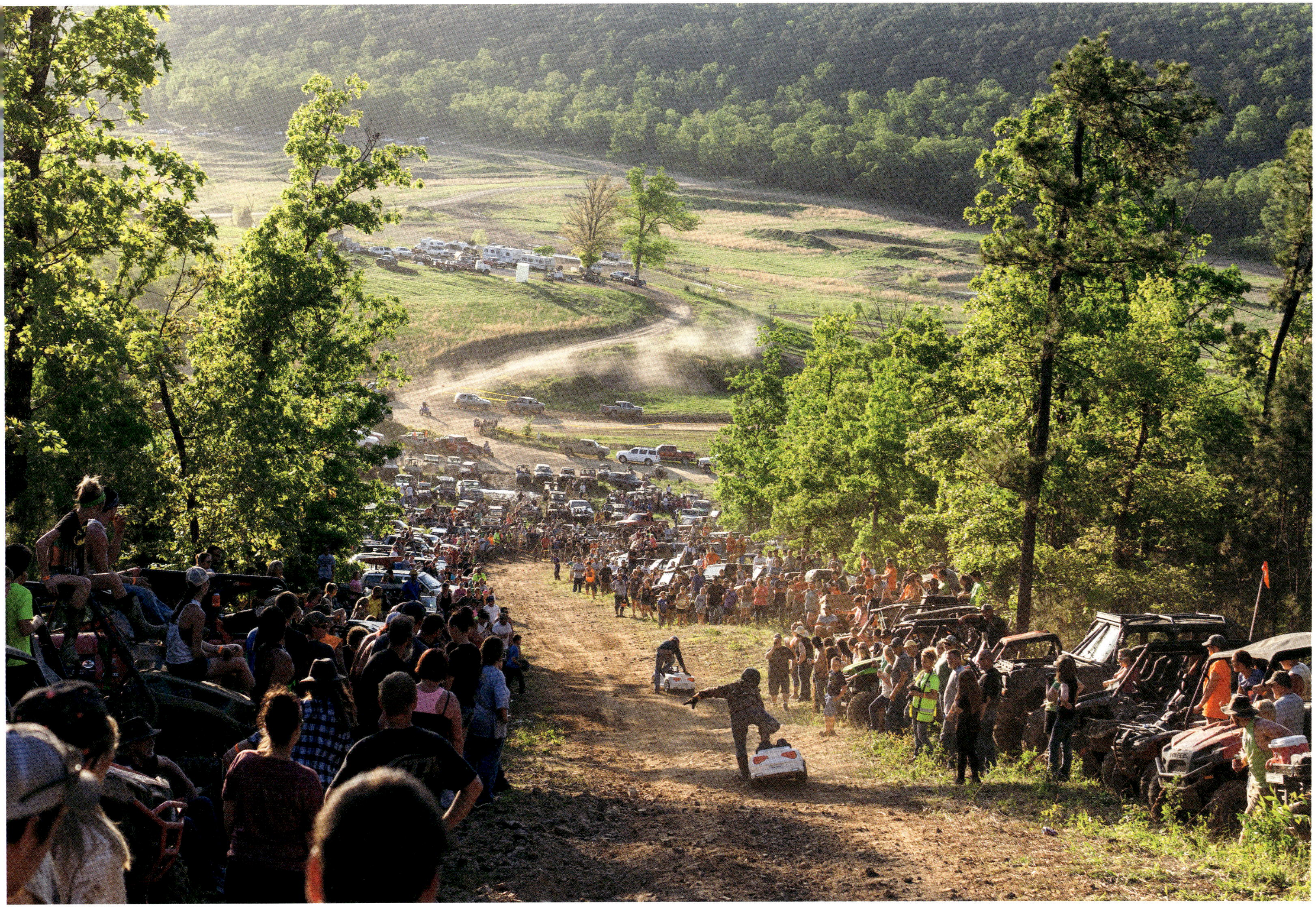

Extreme Barbie Jeep Racing

Booneville, Arkansas, USA

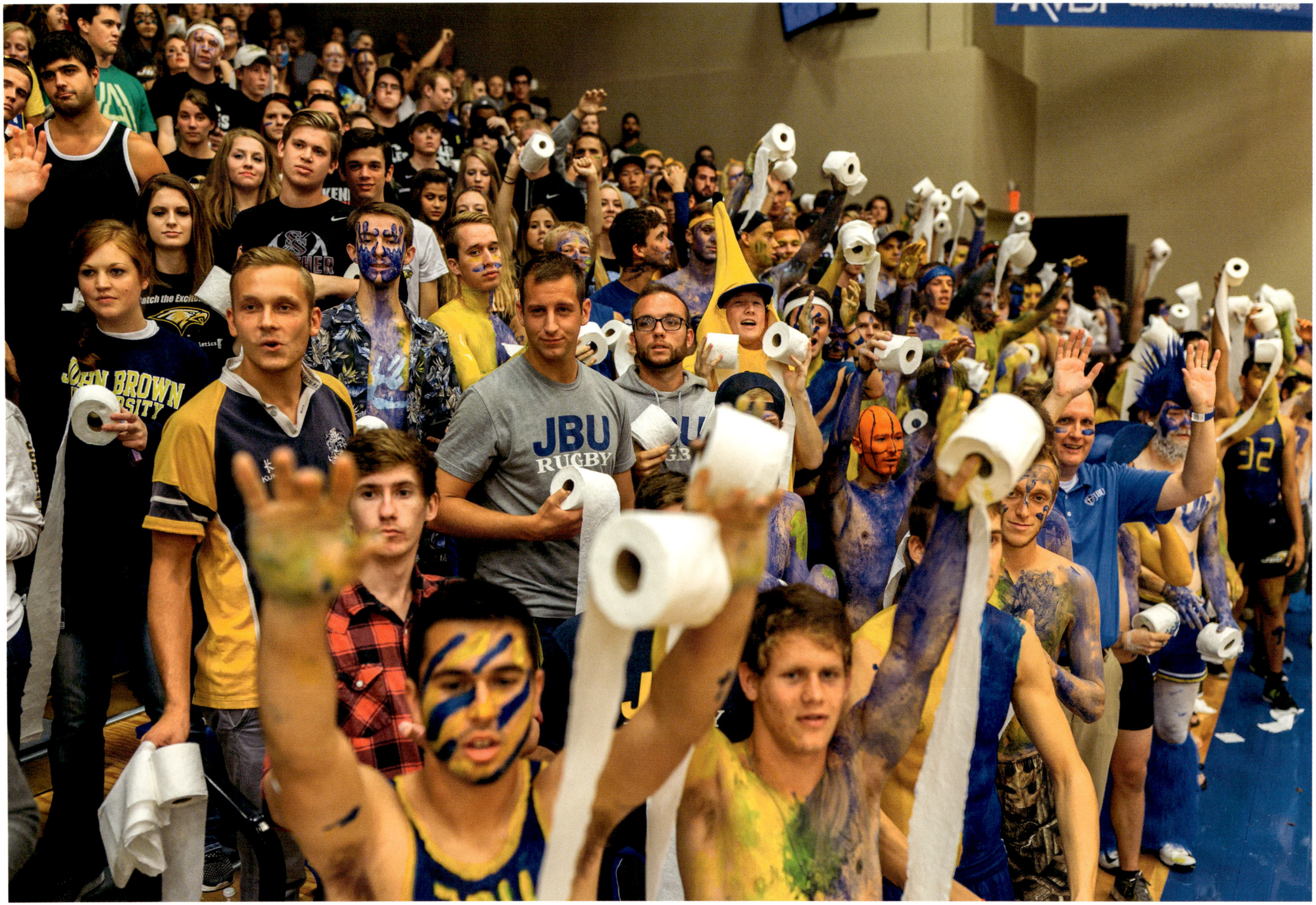

Toilet Paper Game

Siloam Springs, Arkansas, USA

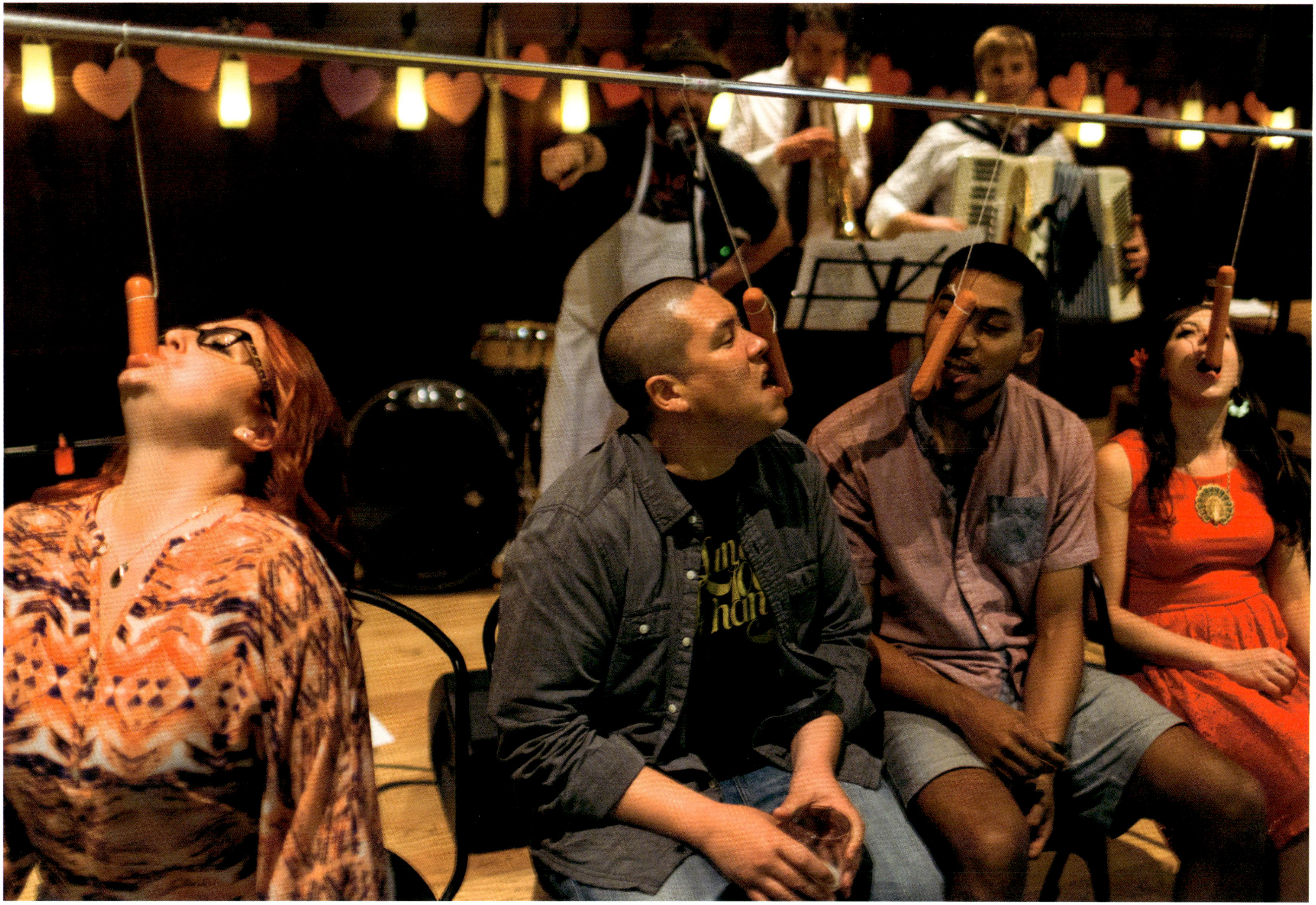

Hot Dog Eating Contest

San Francisco, California, USA

Medieval Rugby

Florence, Italy

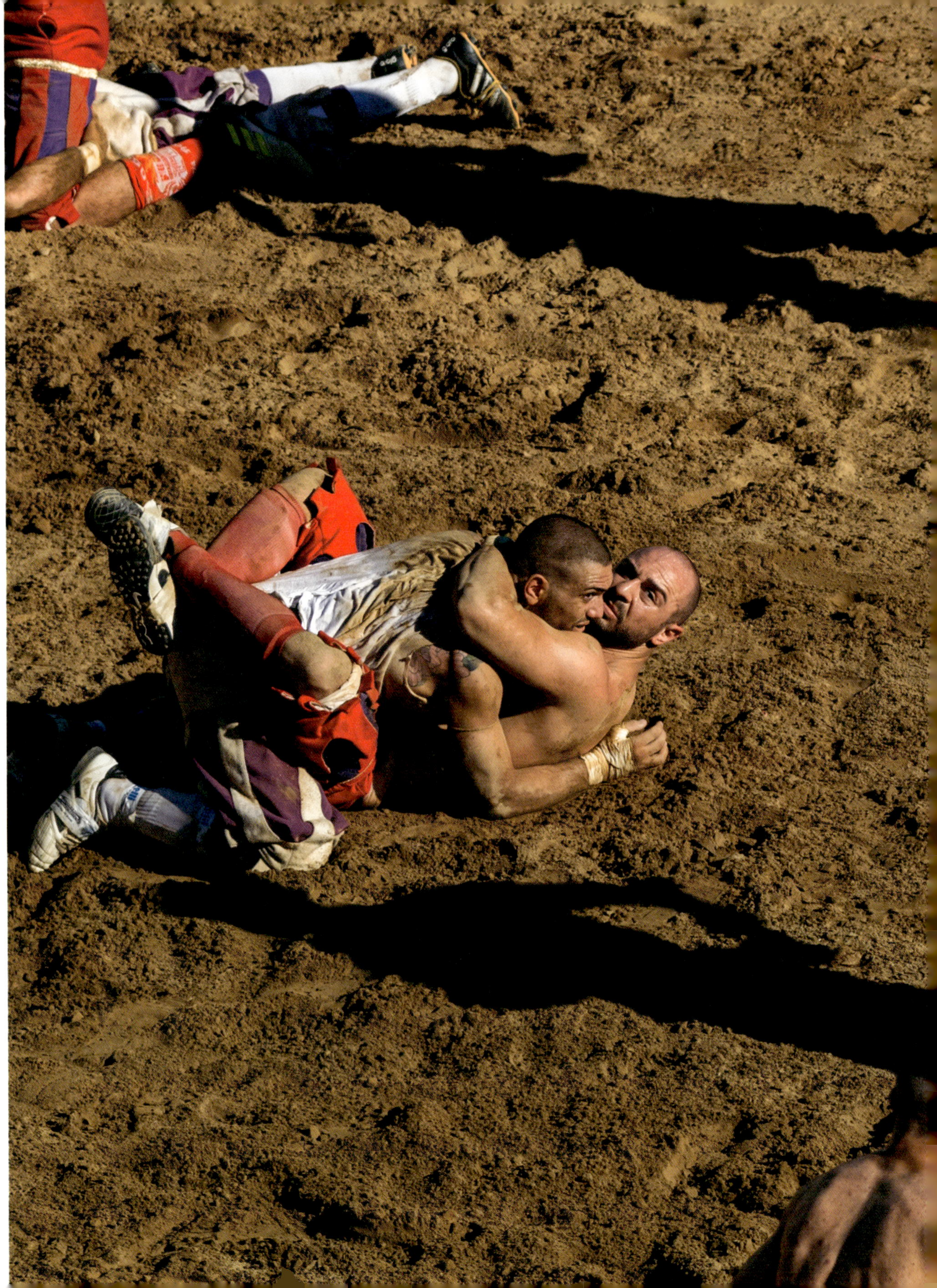

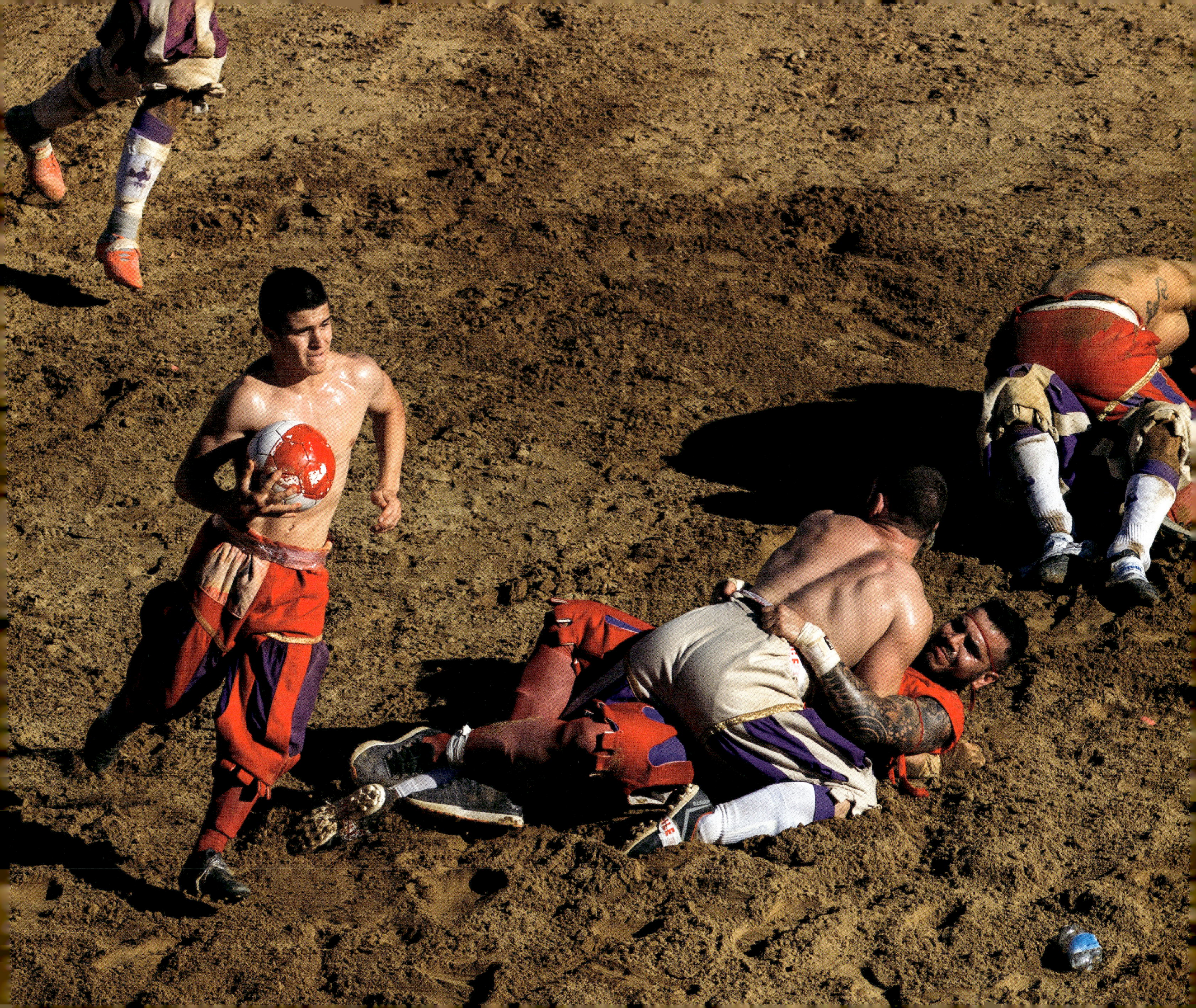

Medieval Rugby

Florence, Italy

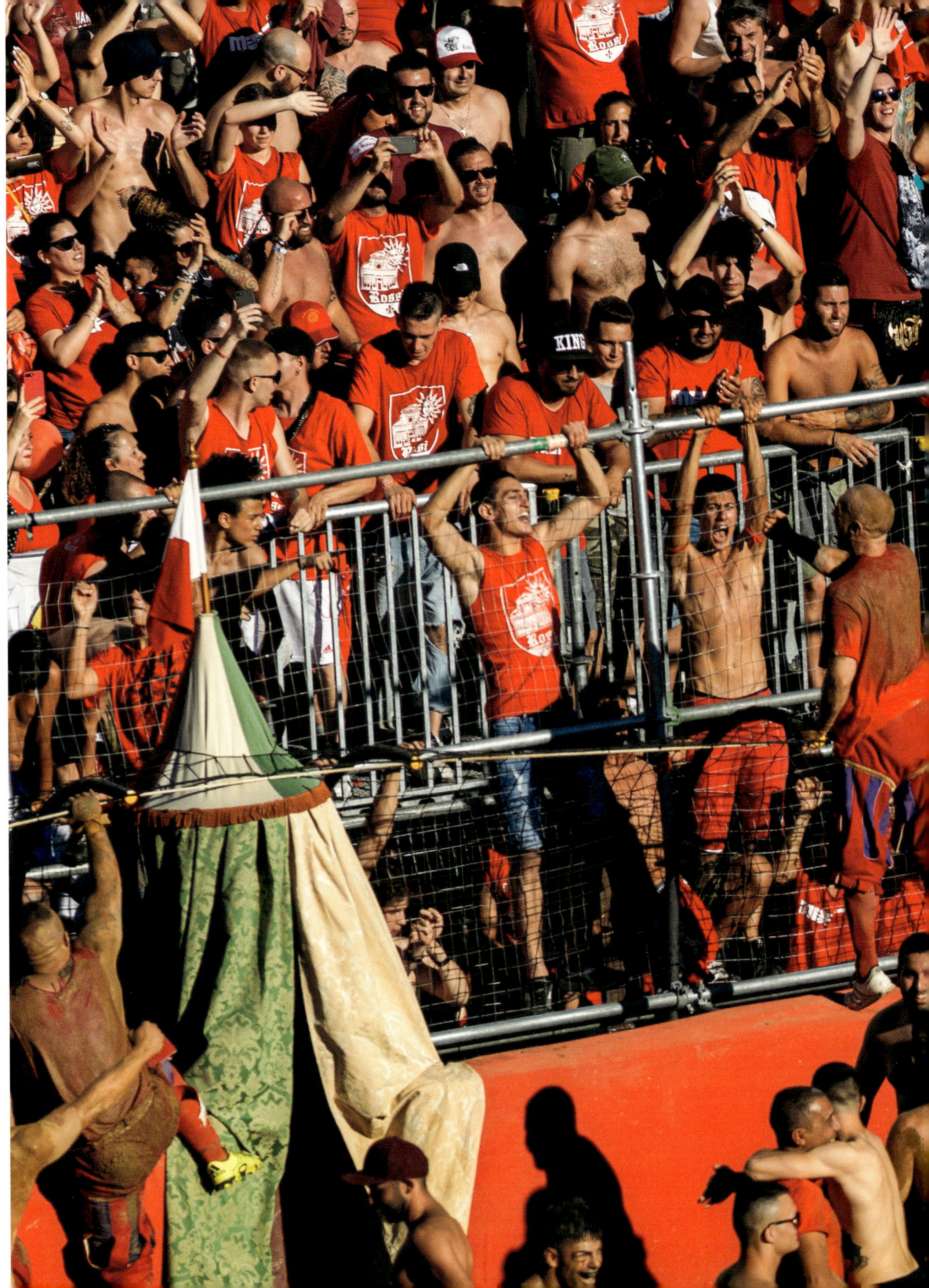

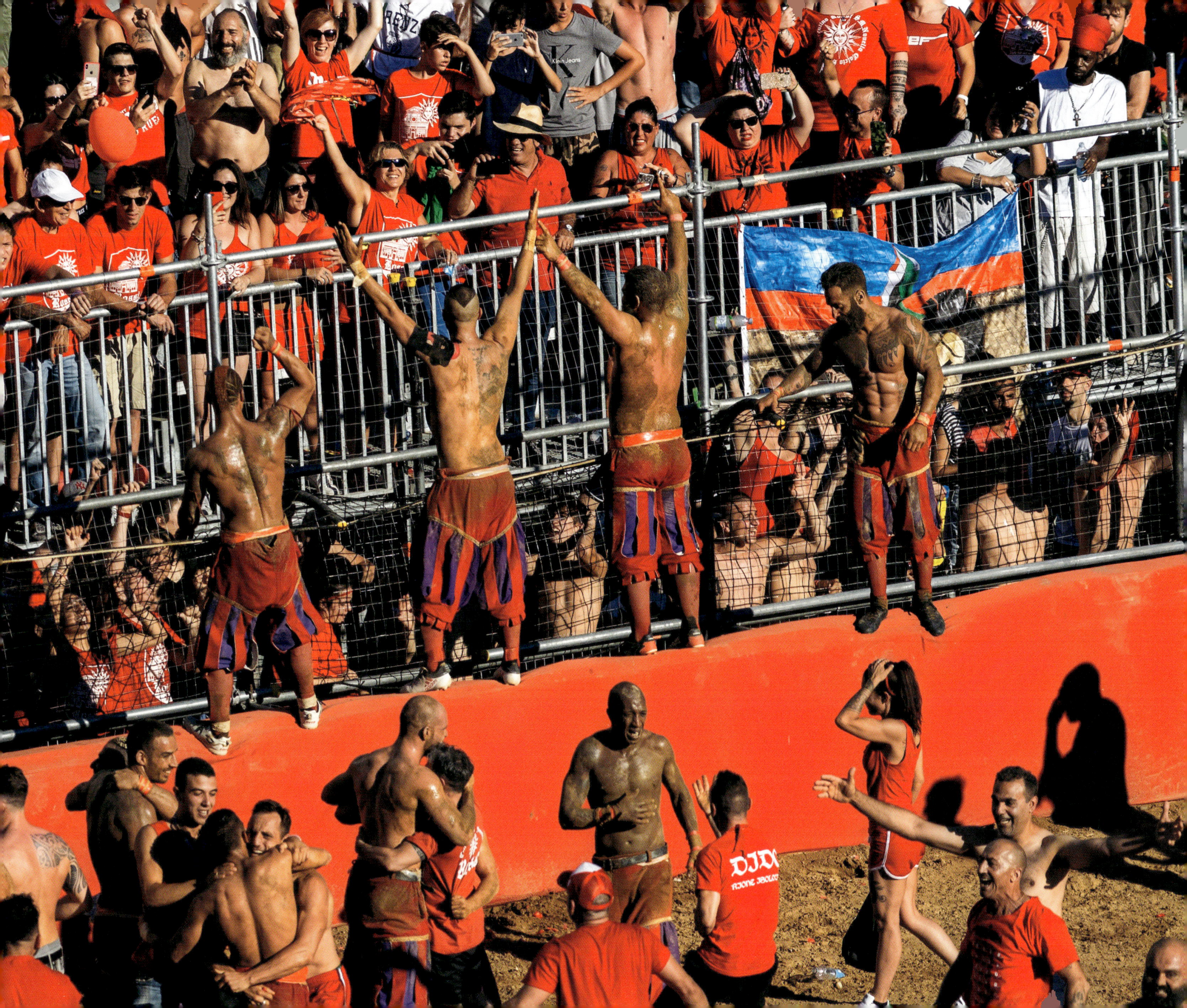

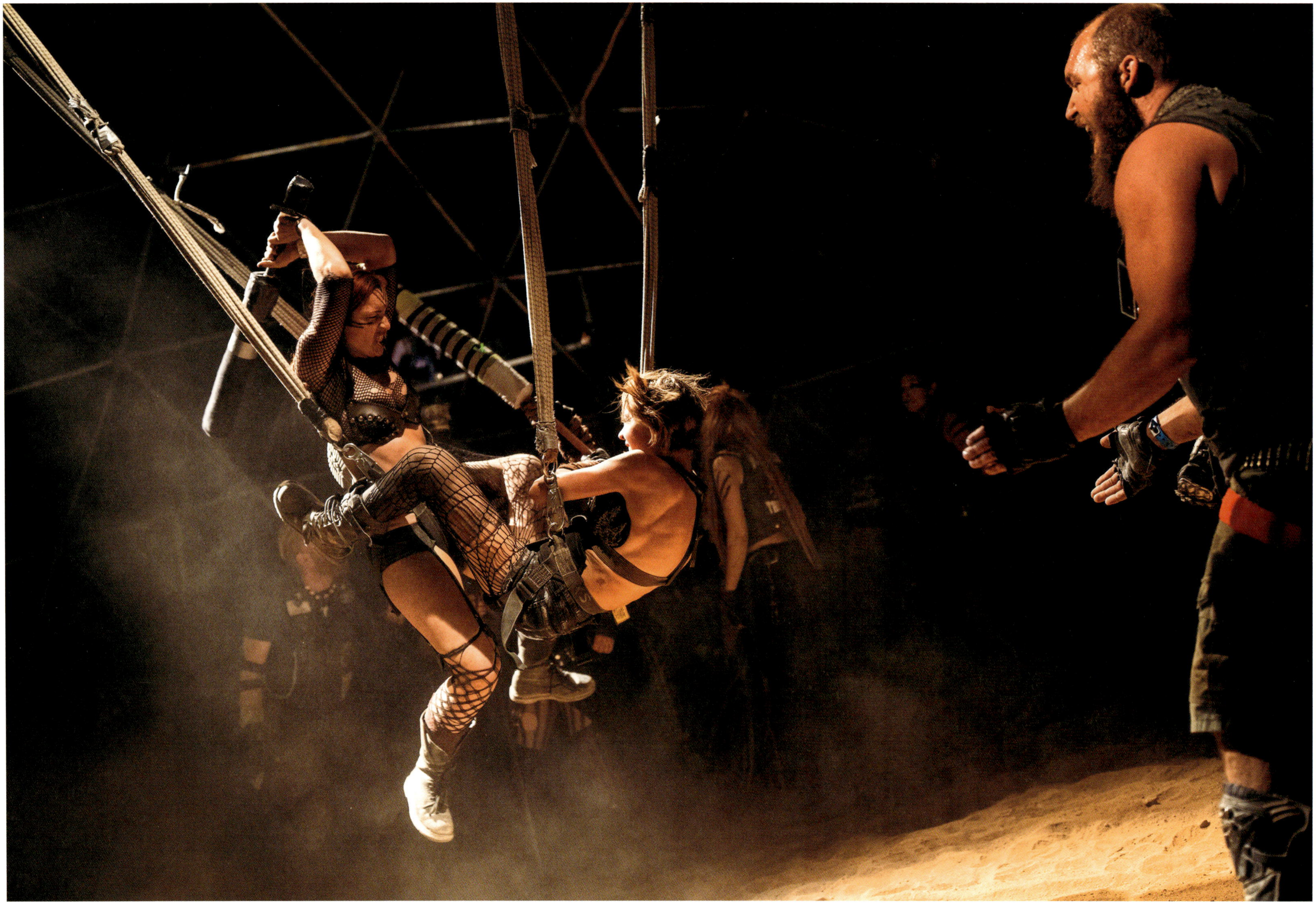

Thunderdome at Wasteland Weekend

Edwards, California, USA

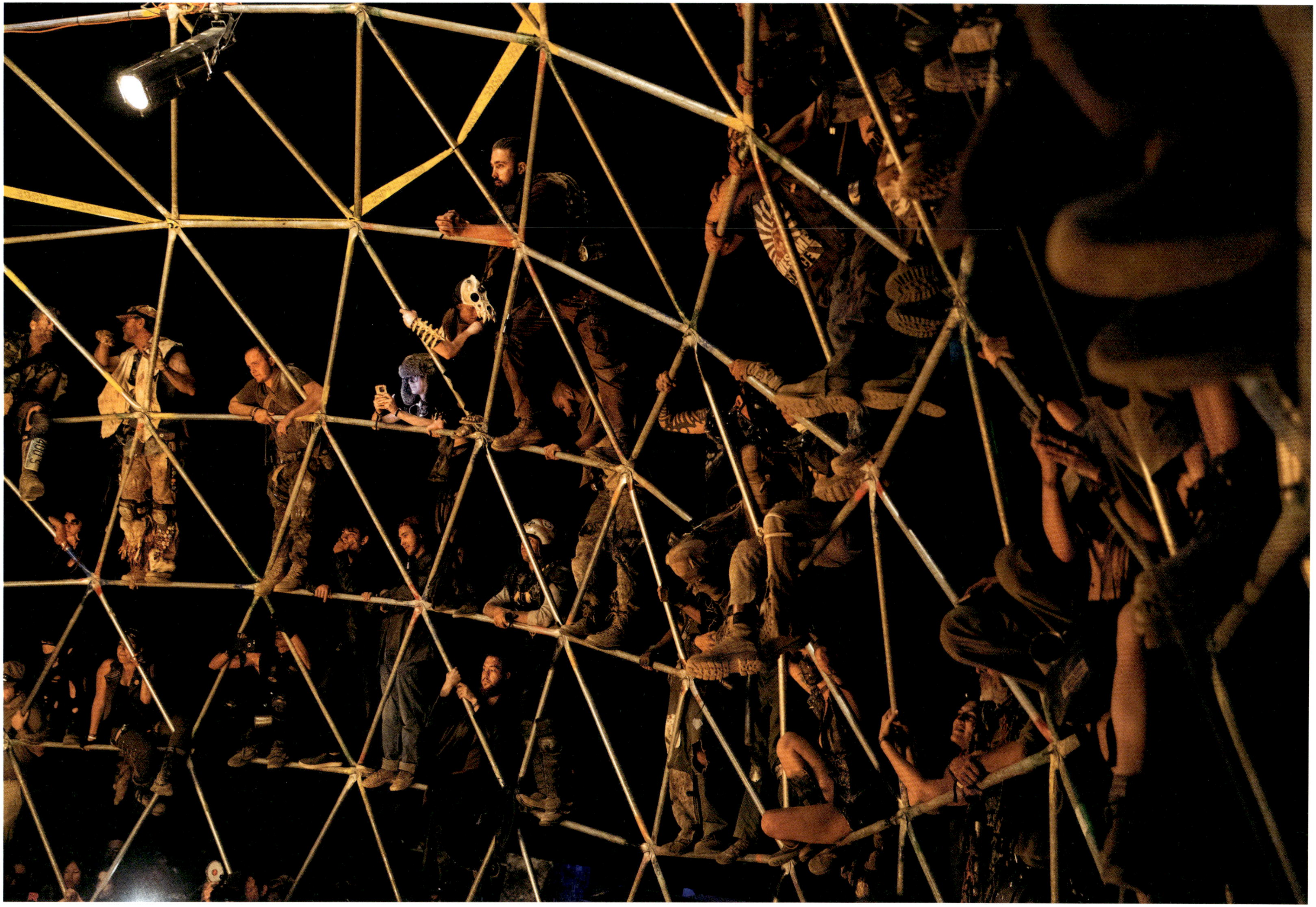

Thunderdome at Wasteland Weekend

Edwards, California, USA

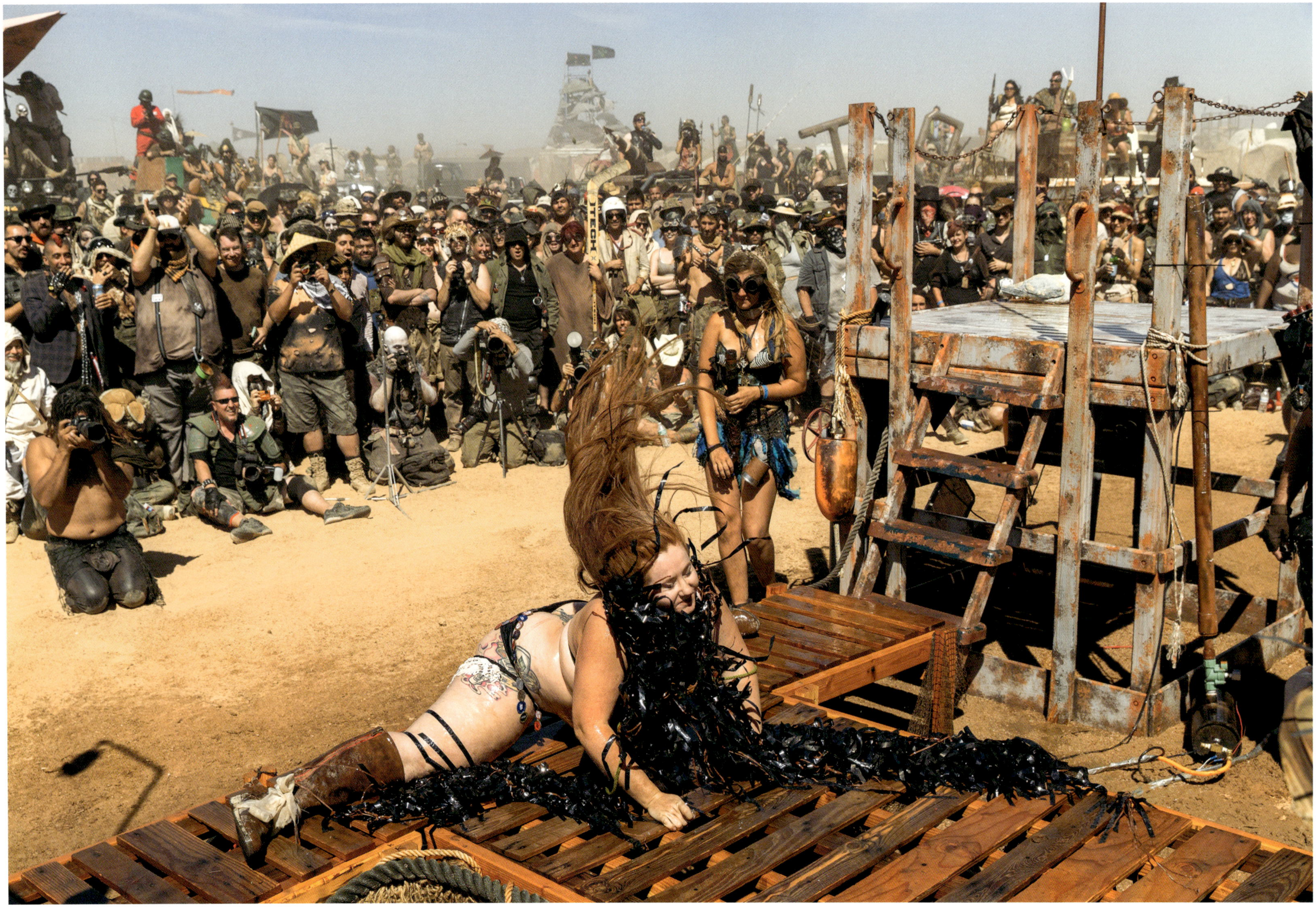

Wasteland Weekend

Edwards, California, USA

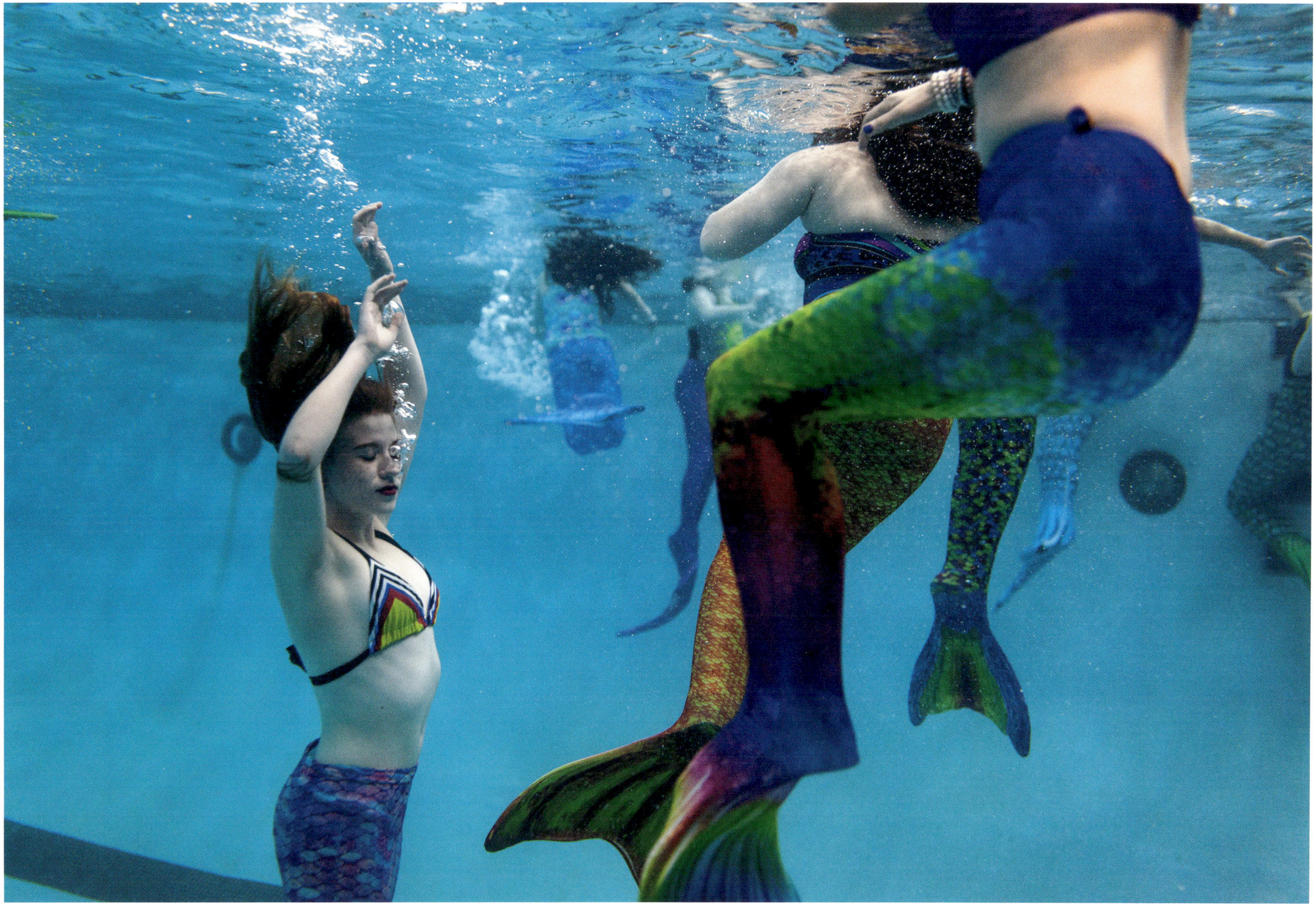

AquaMermaid School

Chicago, Illinois, USA

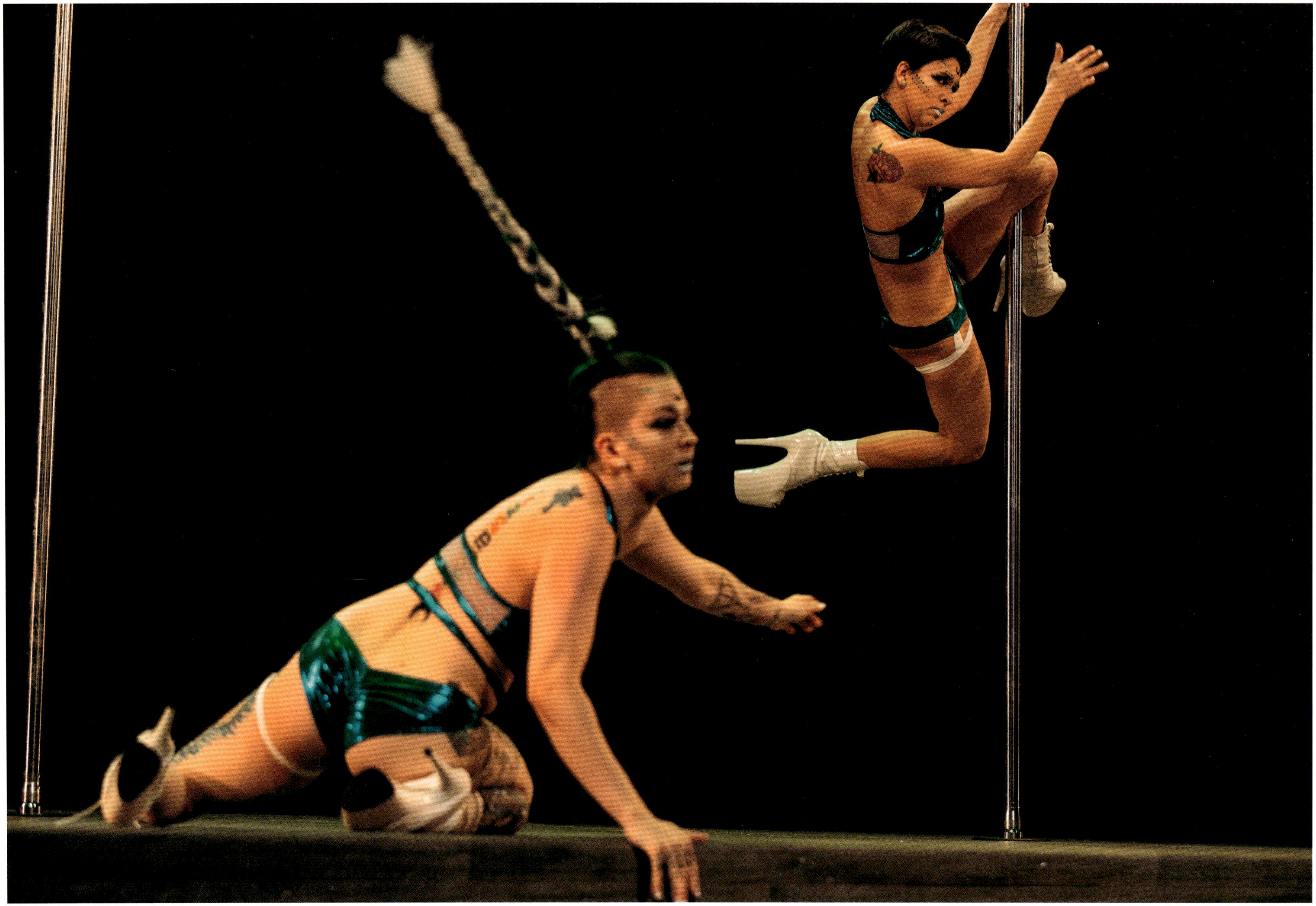

U.S. Pole Dance Championship

New York, New York, USA

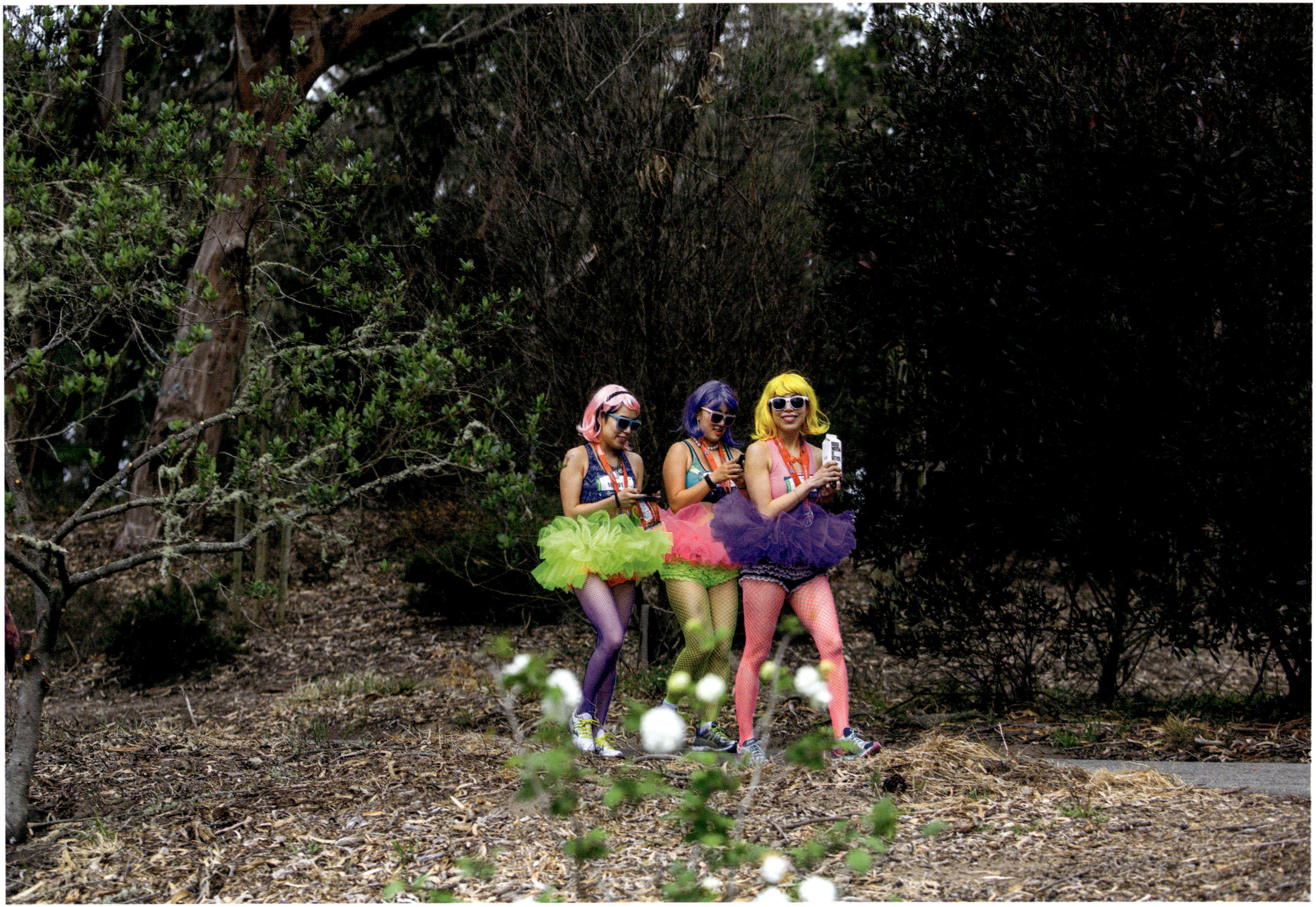

Bay to Breakers

San Francisco, California, USA

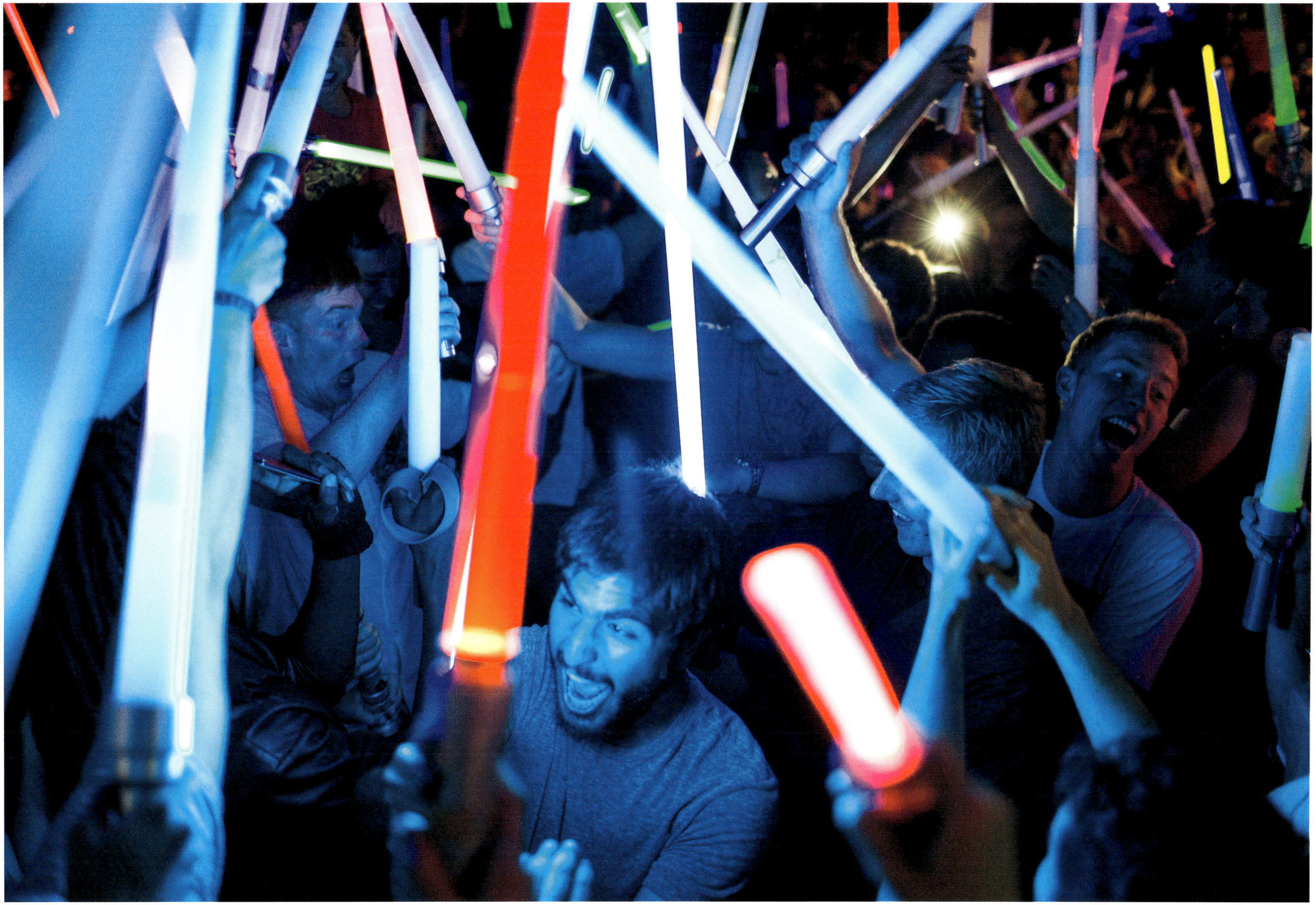

Lightsaber Battle

New York, New York, USA

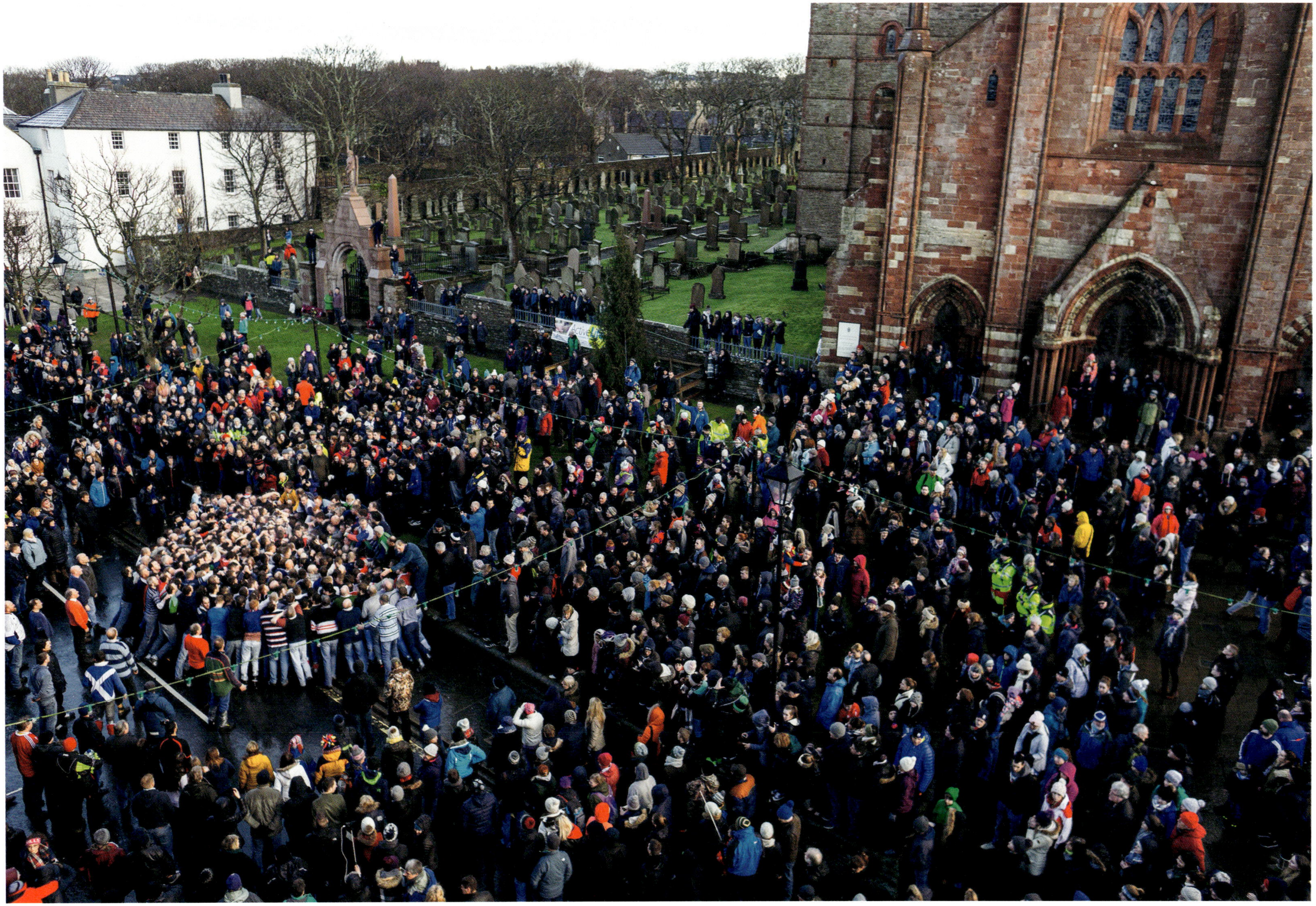

Mob Soccer

Kirkwall, Scotland, UK

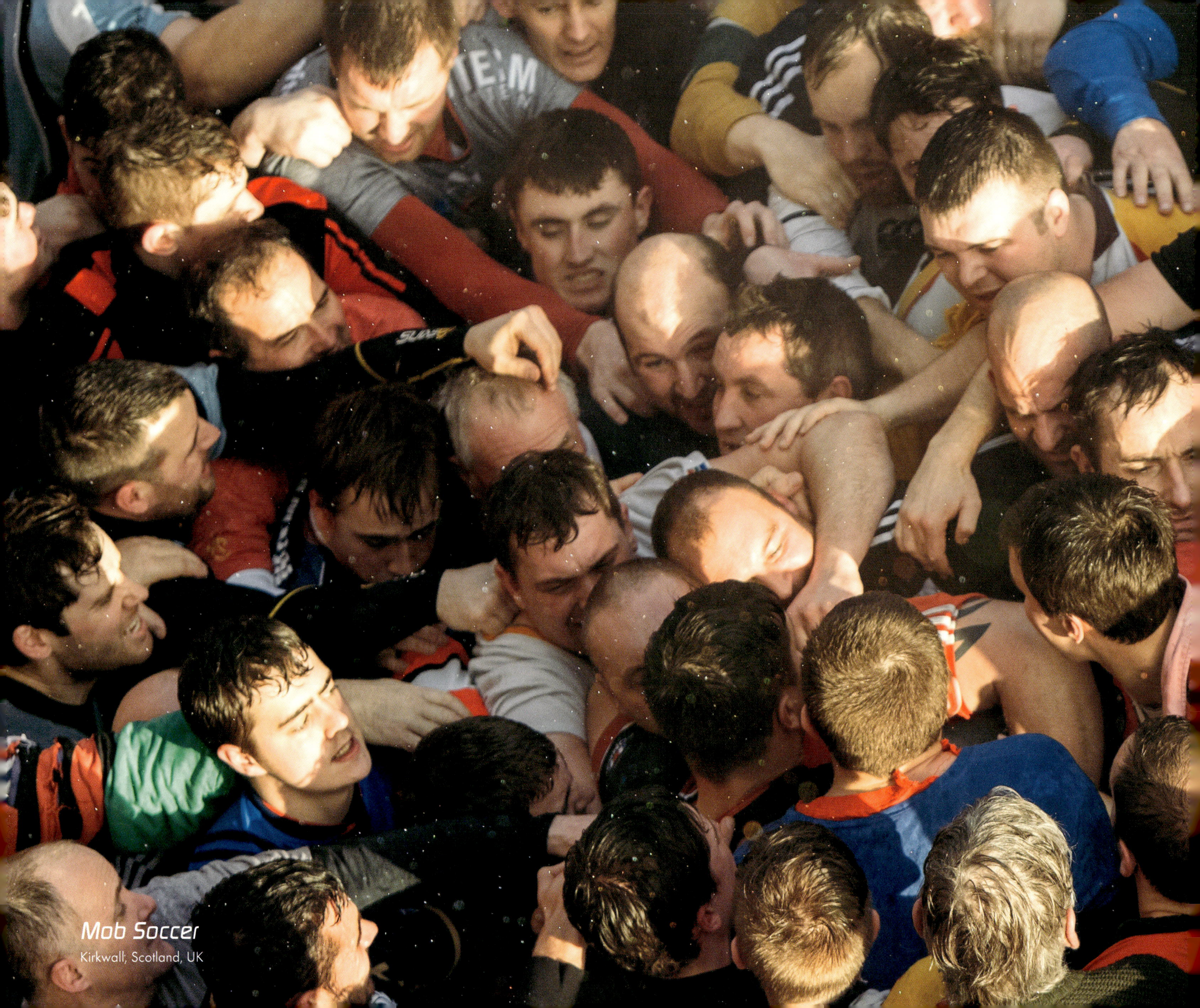

Mob Soccer

Kirkwall, Scotland, UK

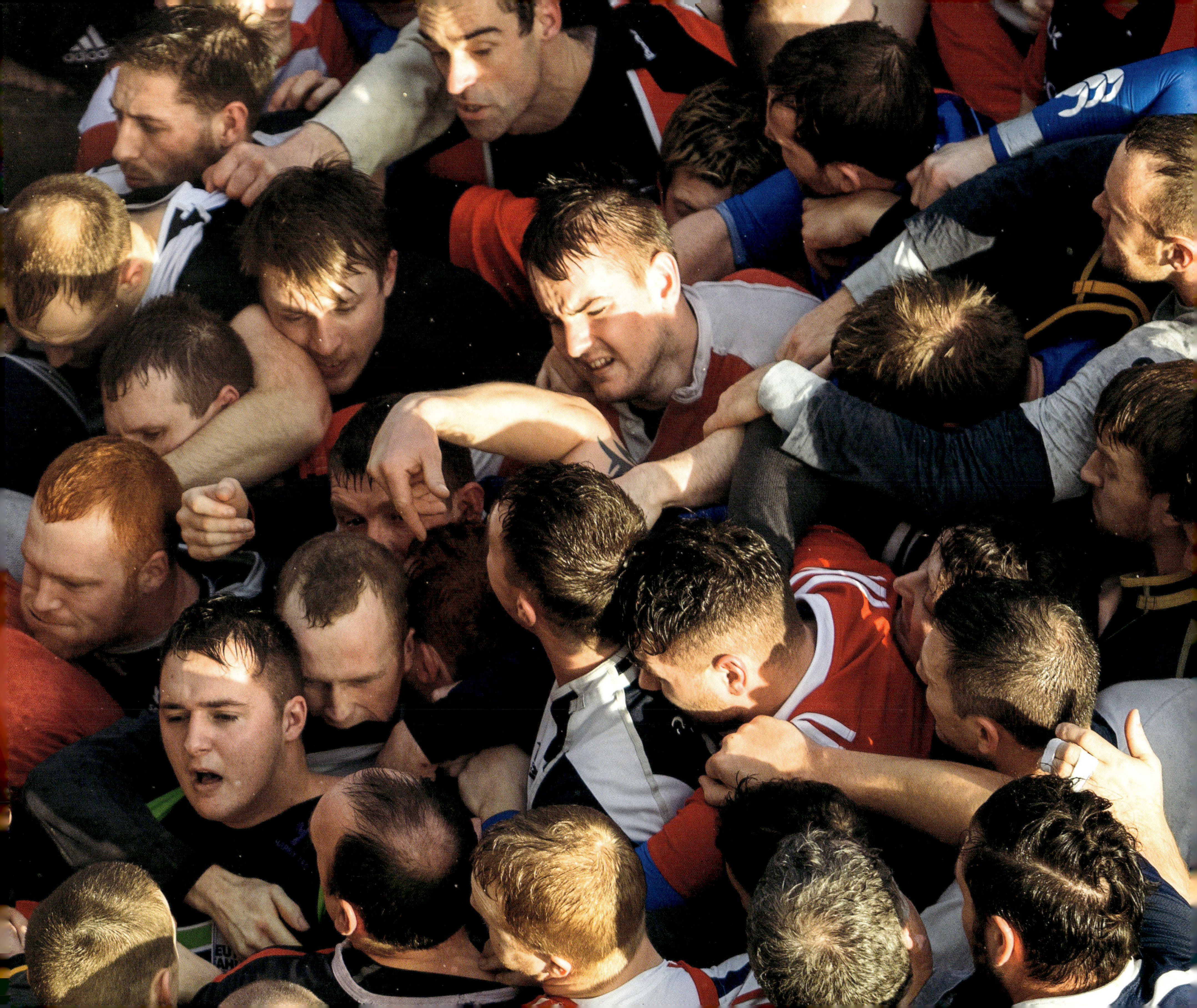

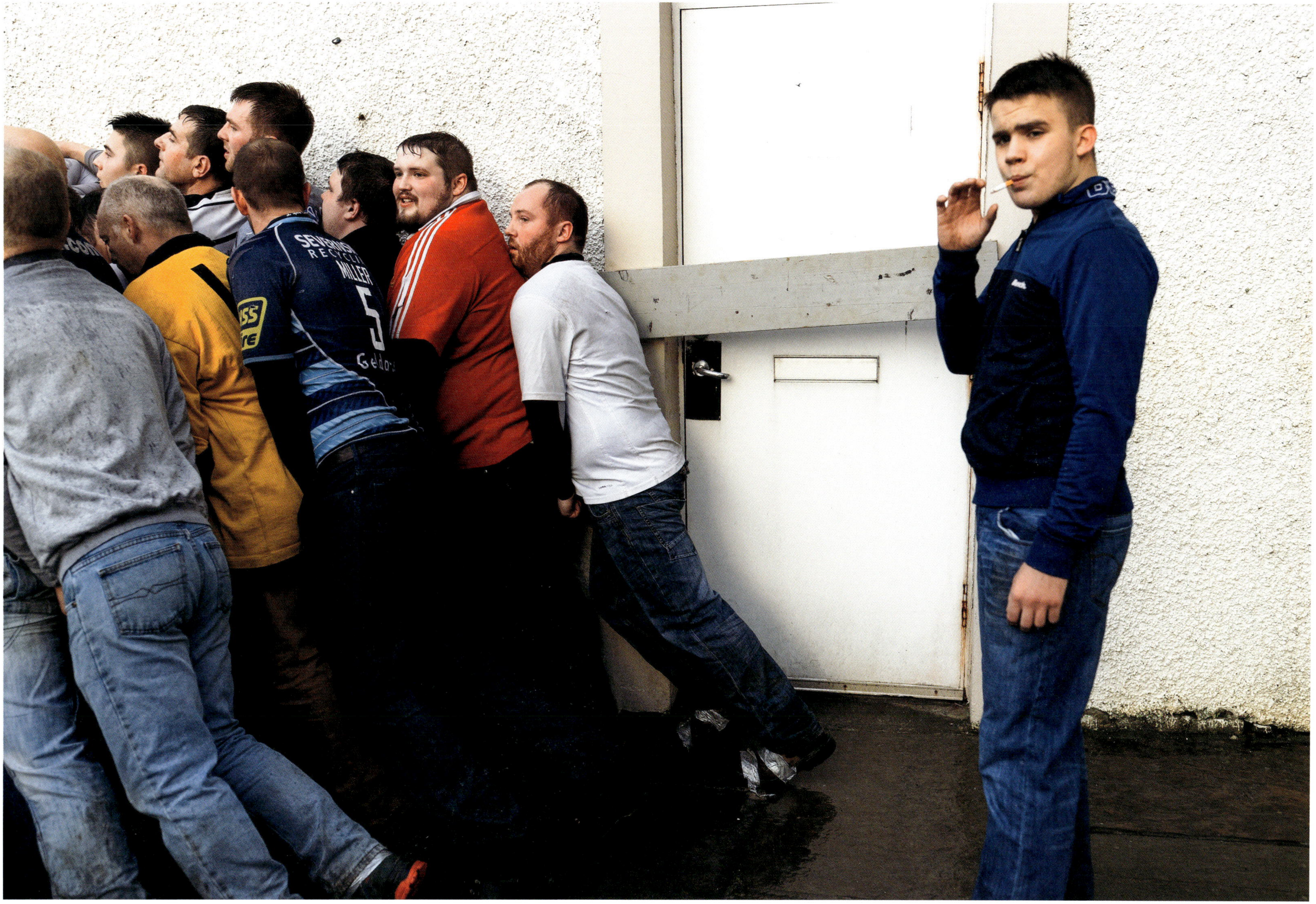

Mob Soccer

Kirkwall, Scotland, UK

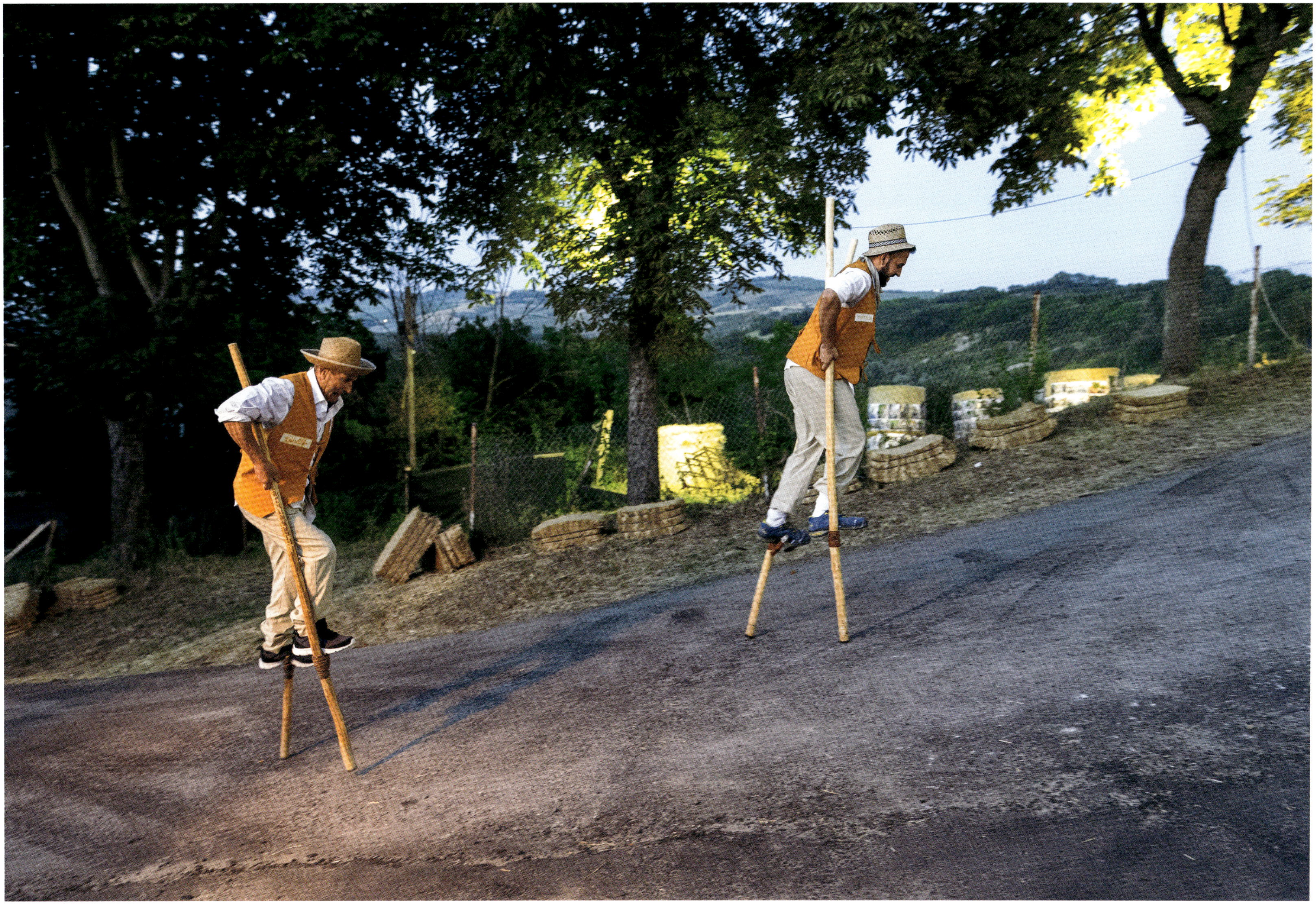

Stilt Racing

Schieti, Italy

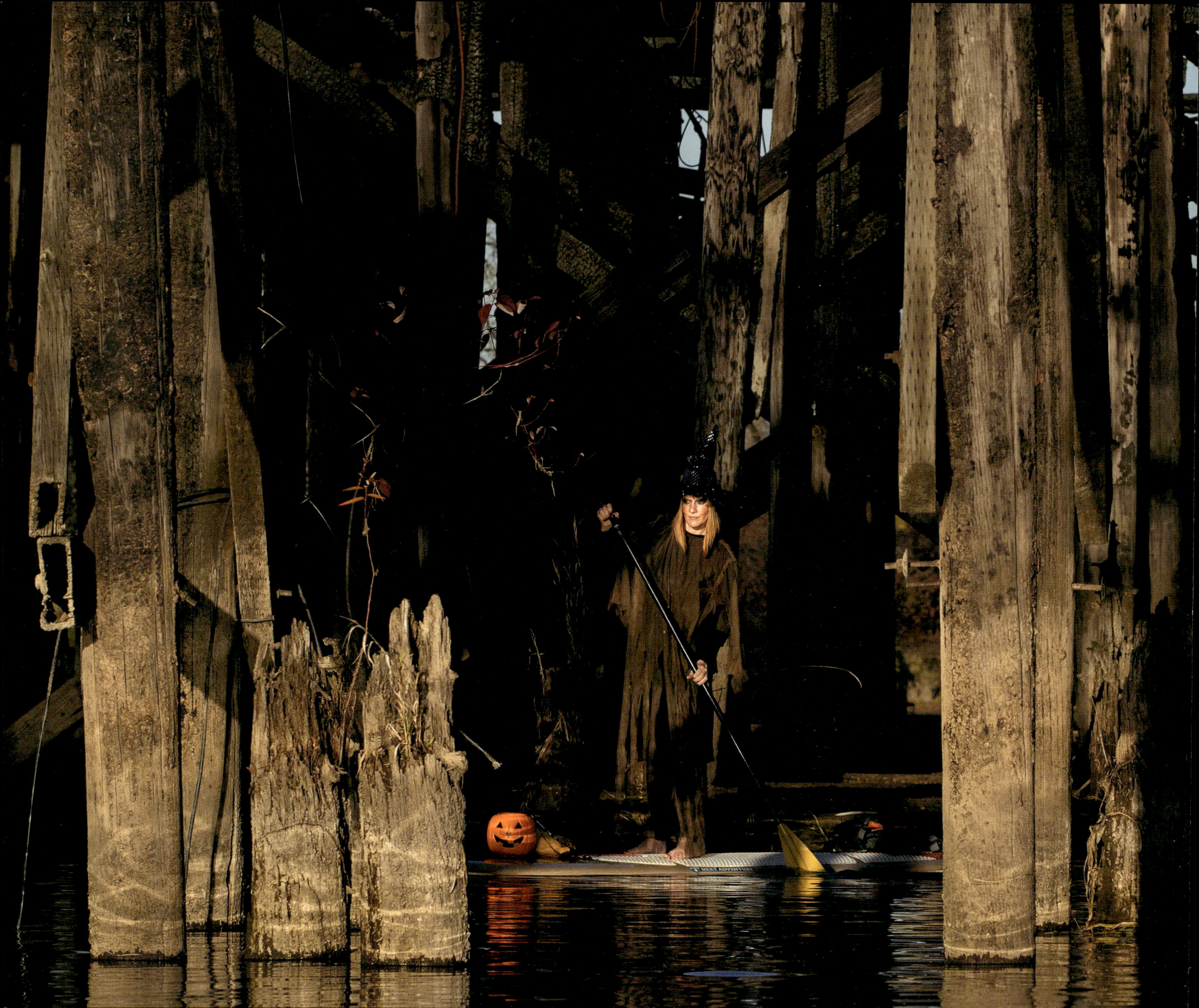

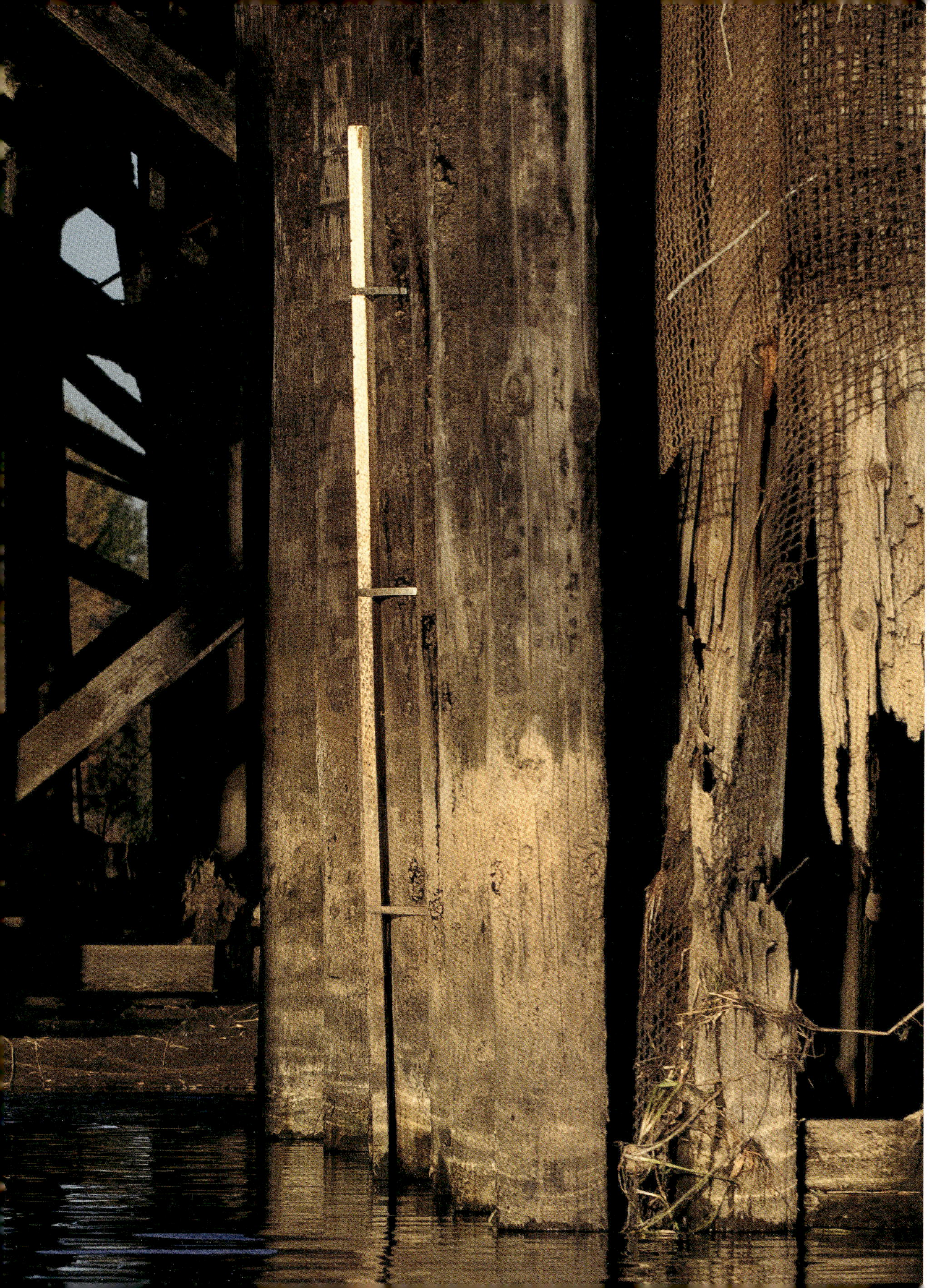

Halloween Witch Paddle

Scappoose, Oregon, USA

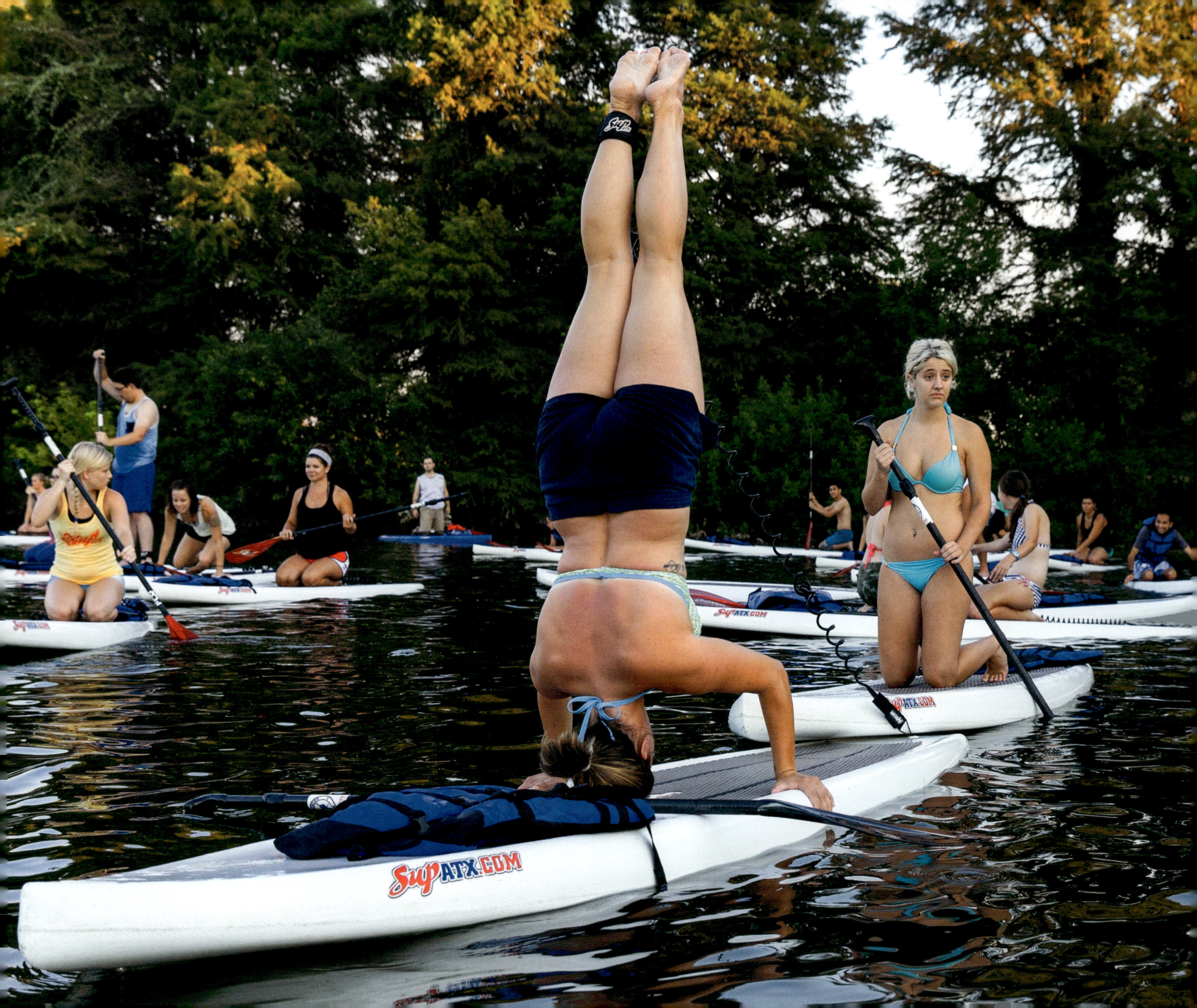
SupATX.COM

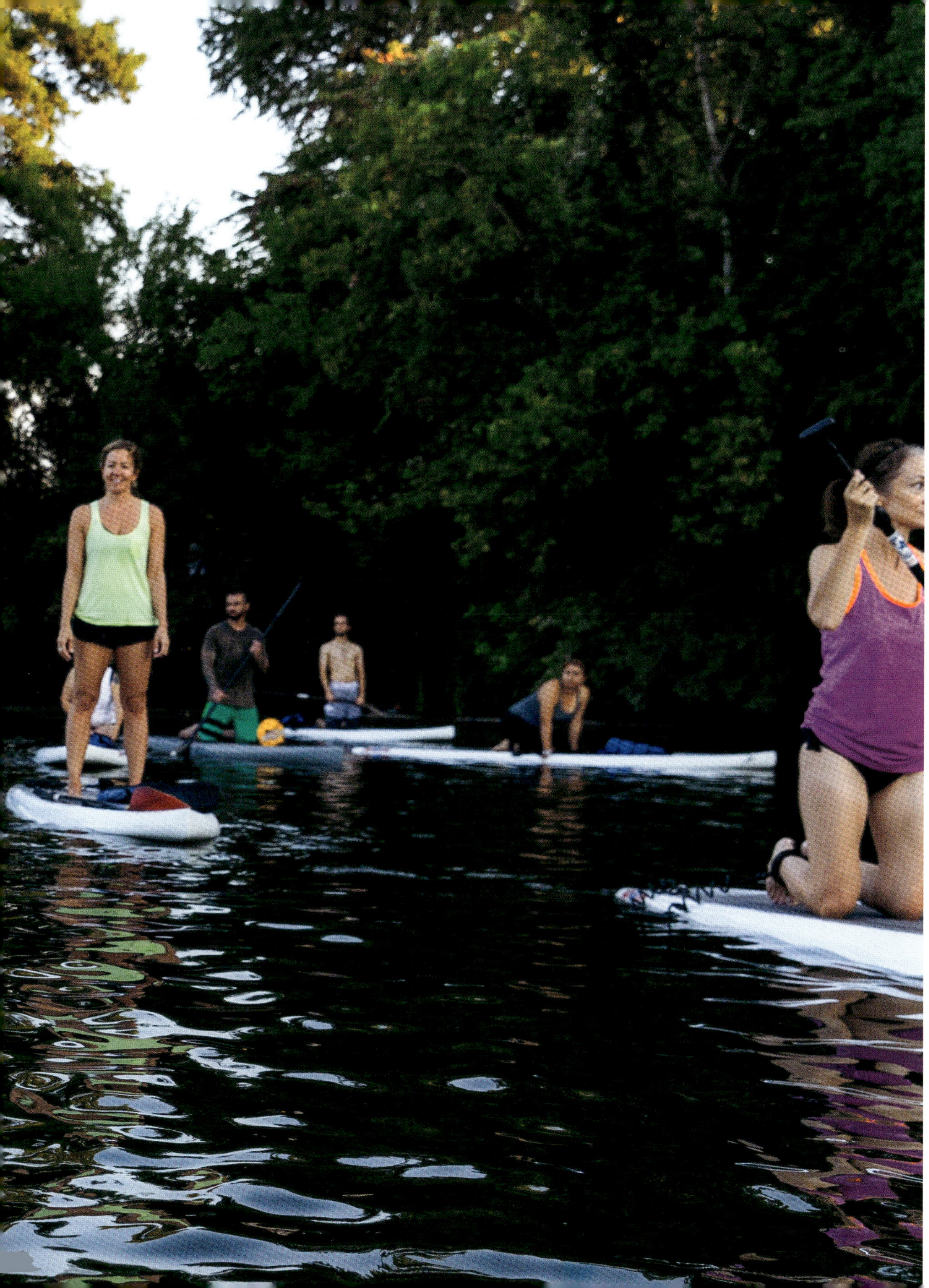

World Record SUP Yoga Class

Austin, Texas, USA

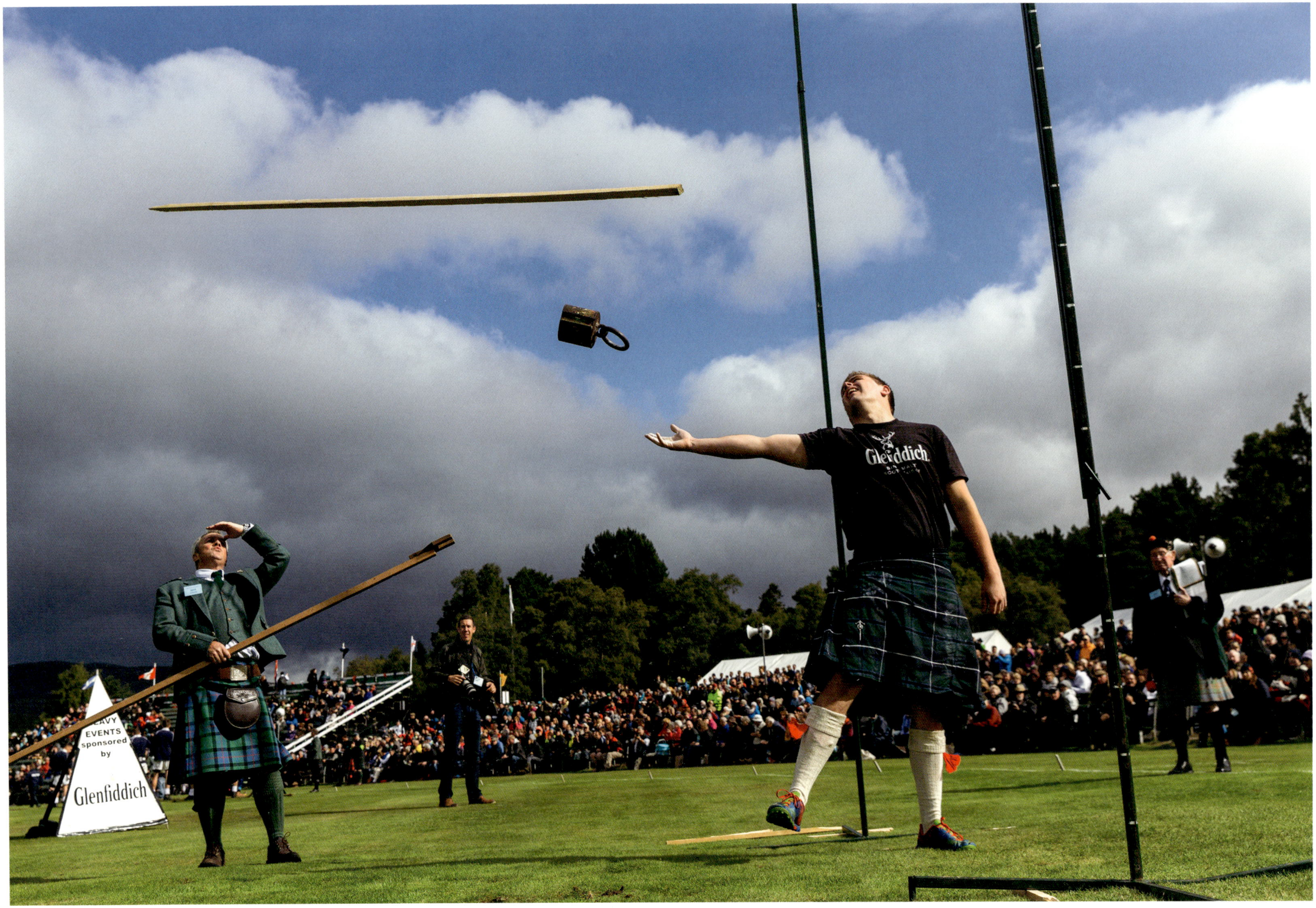

Weight Over Bar

Braemar, Scotland, UK

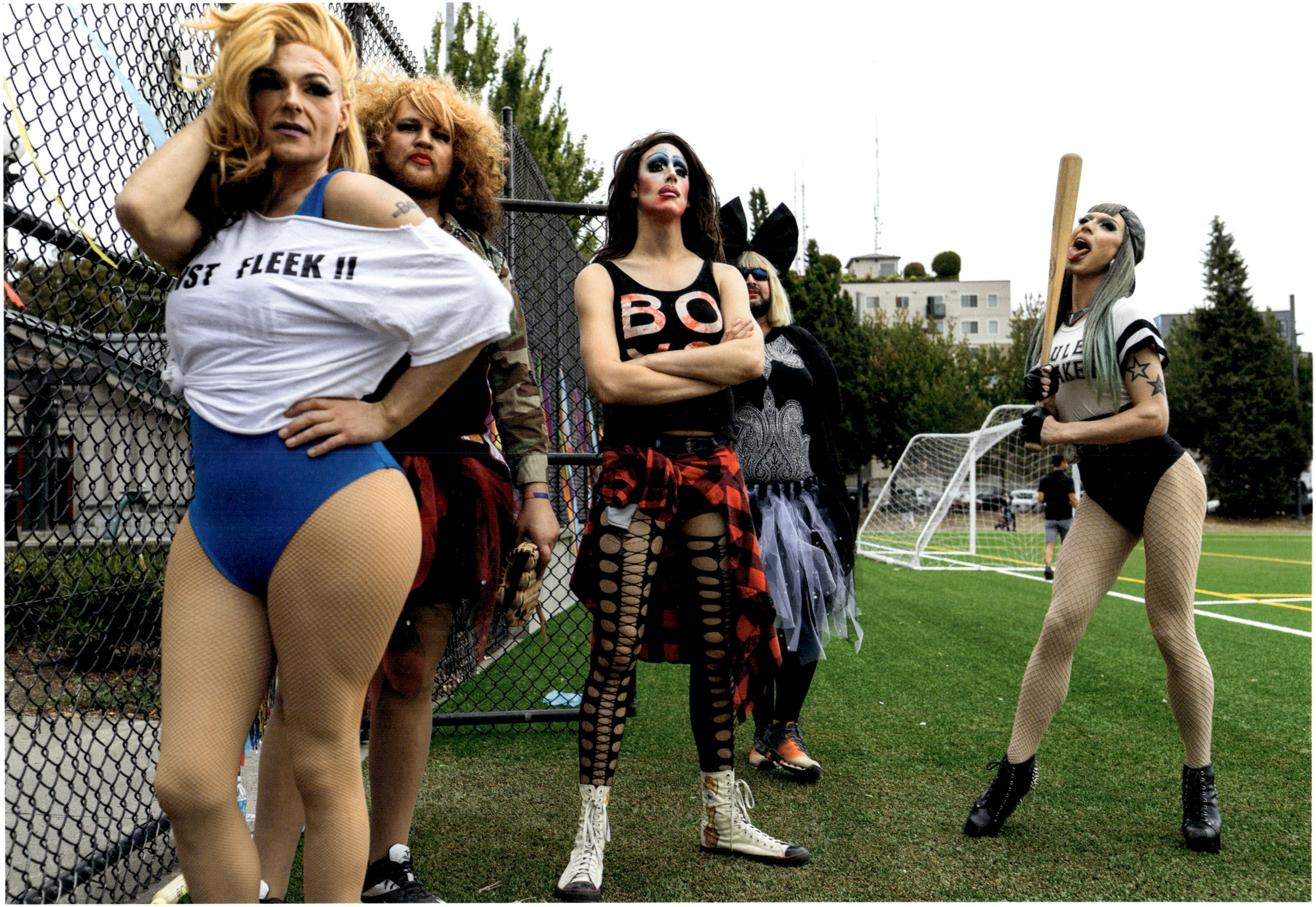

Drag Queen Softball

Seattle, Washington, USA

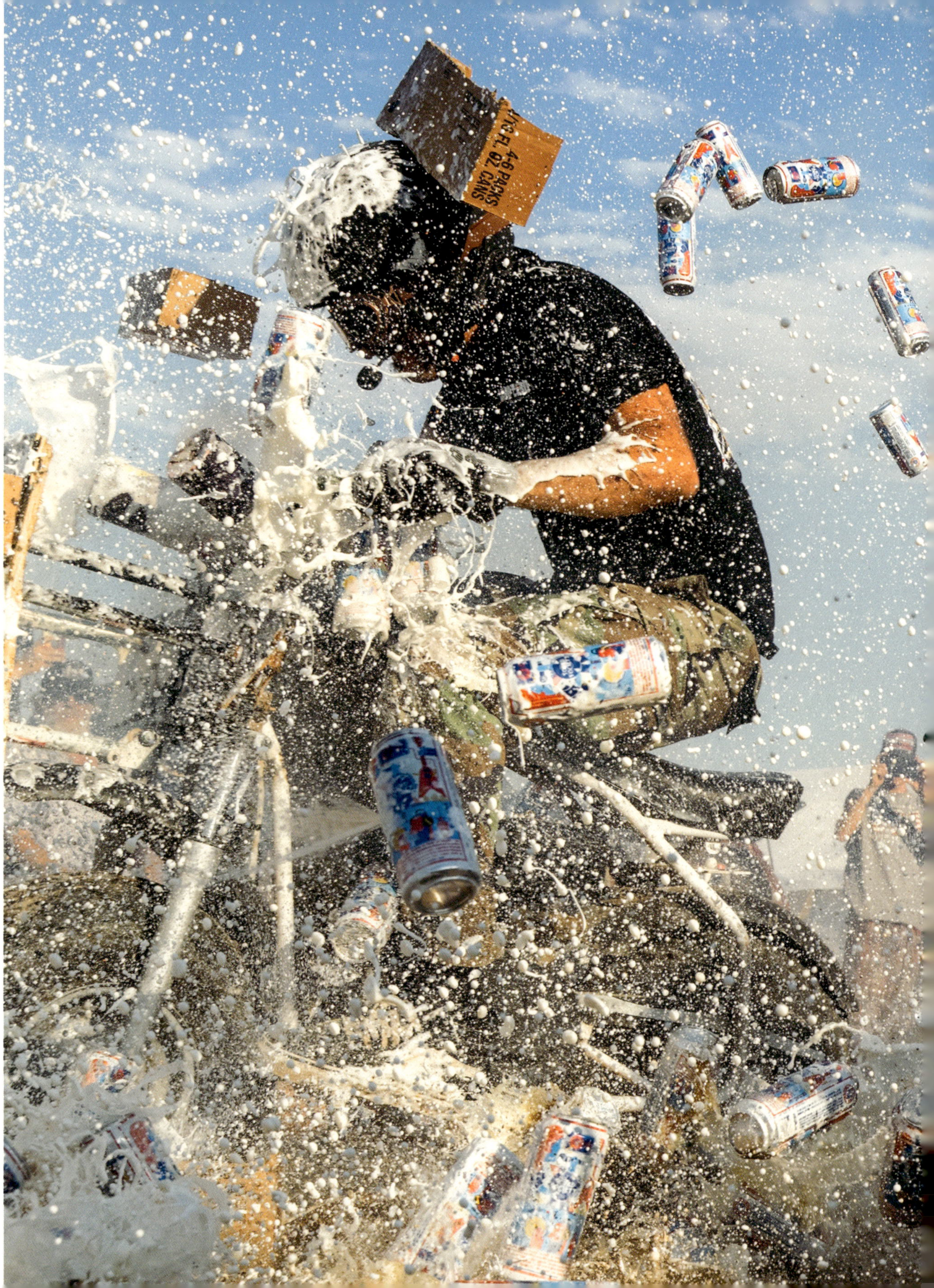

Motorcycle vs. Wall of Beer

Sturgis, South Dakota, USA

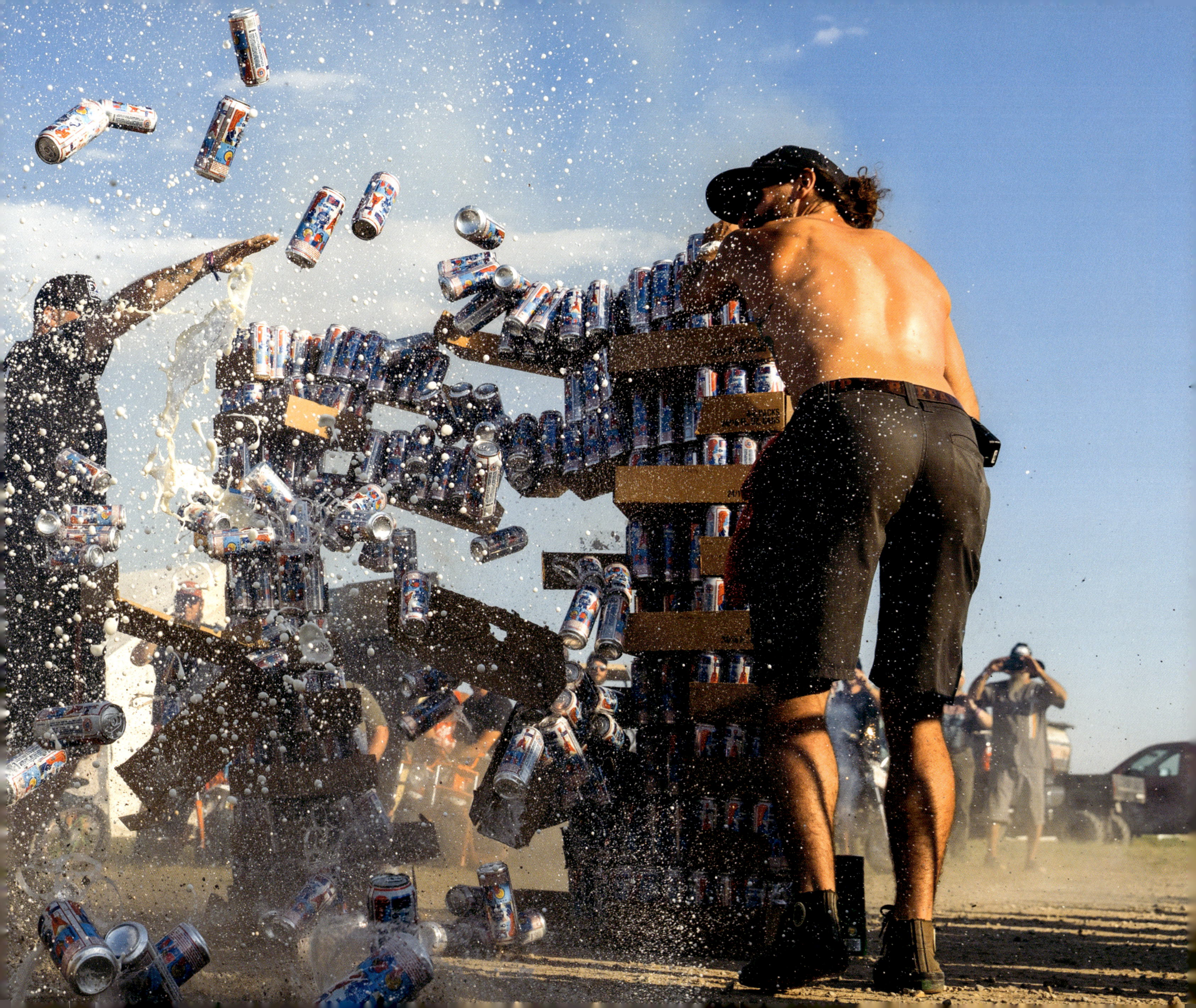

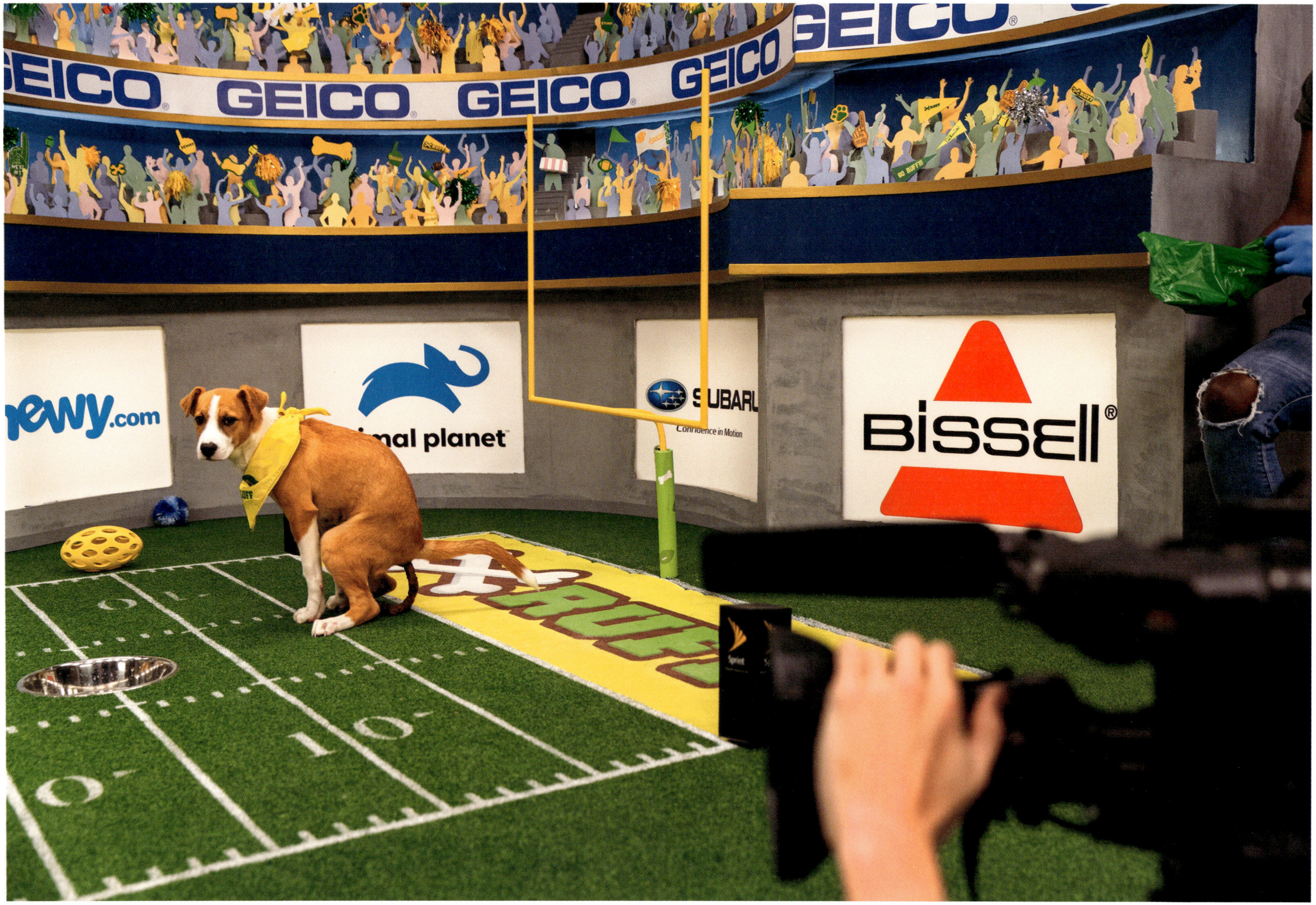

Puppy Bowl

New York, New York, USA

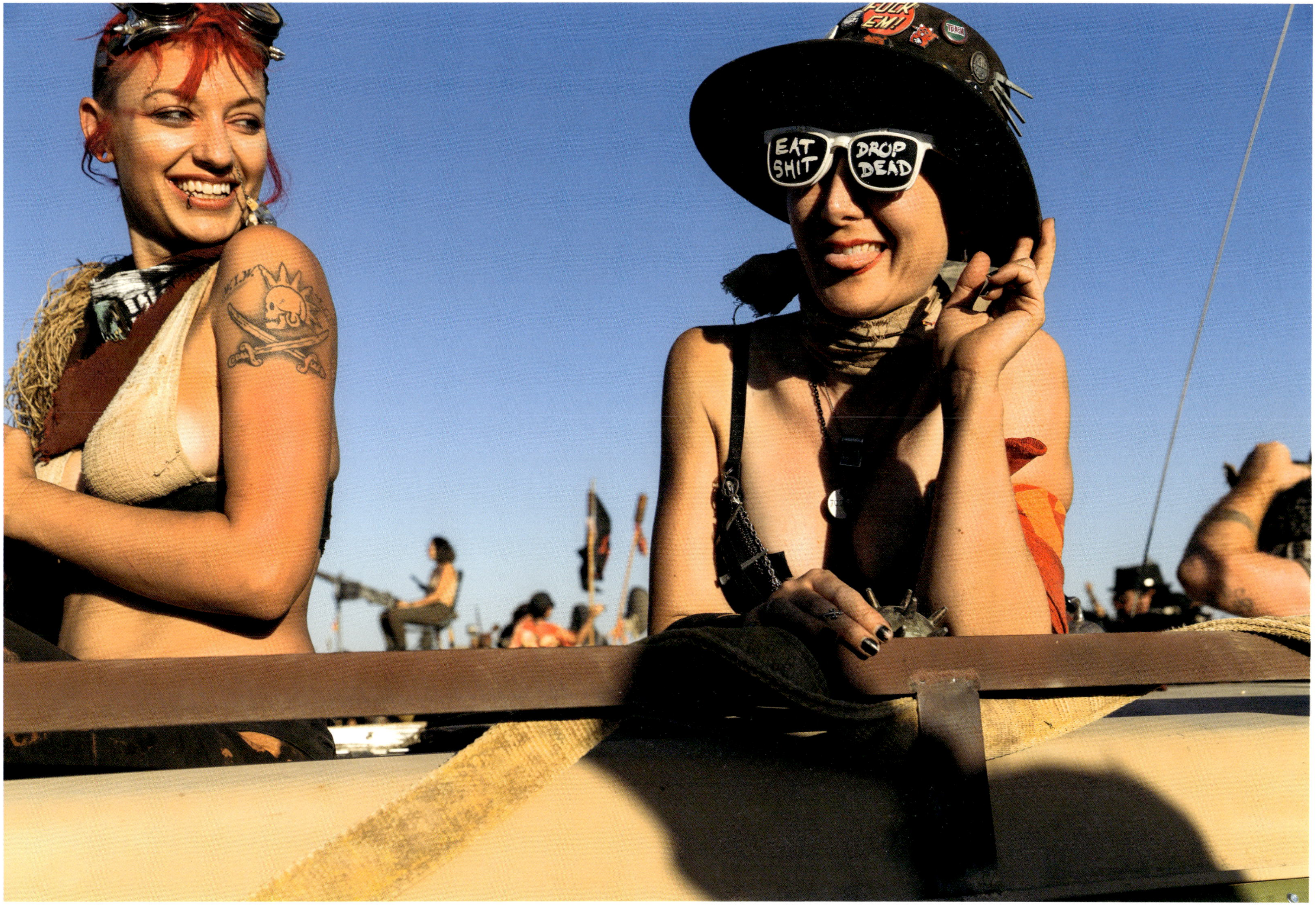

Wasteland Weekend

Edwards, California, USA

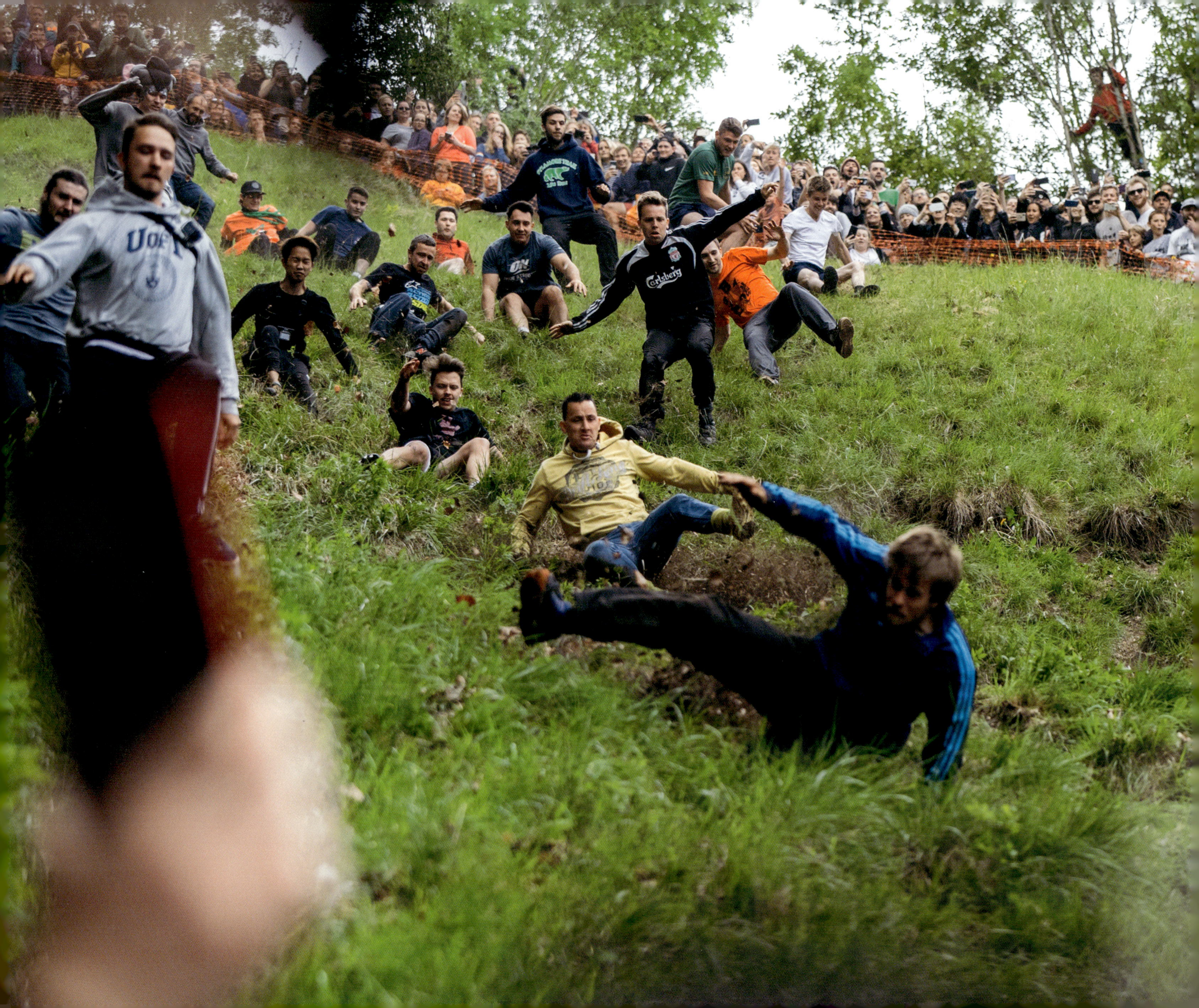
Carlsberg

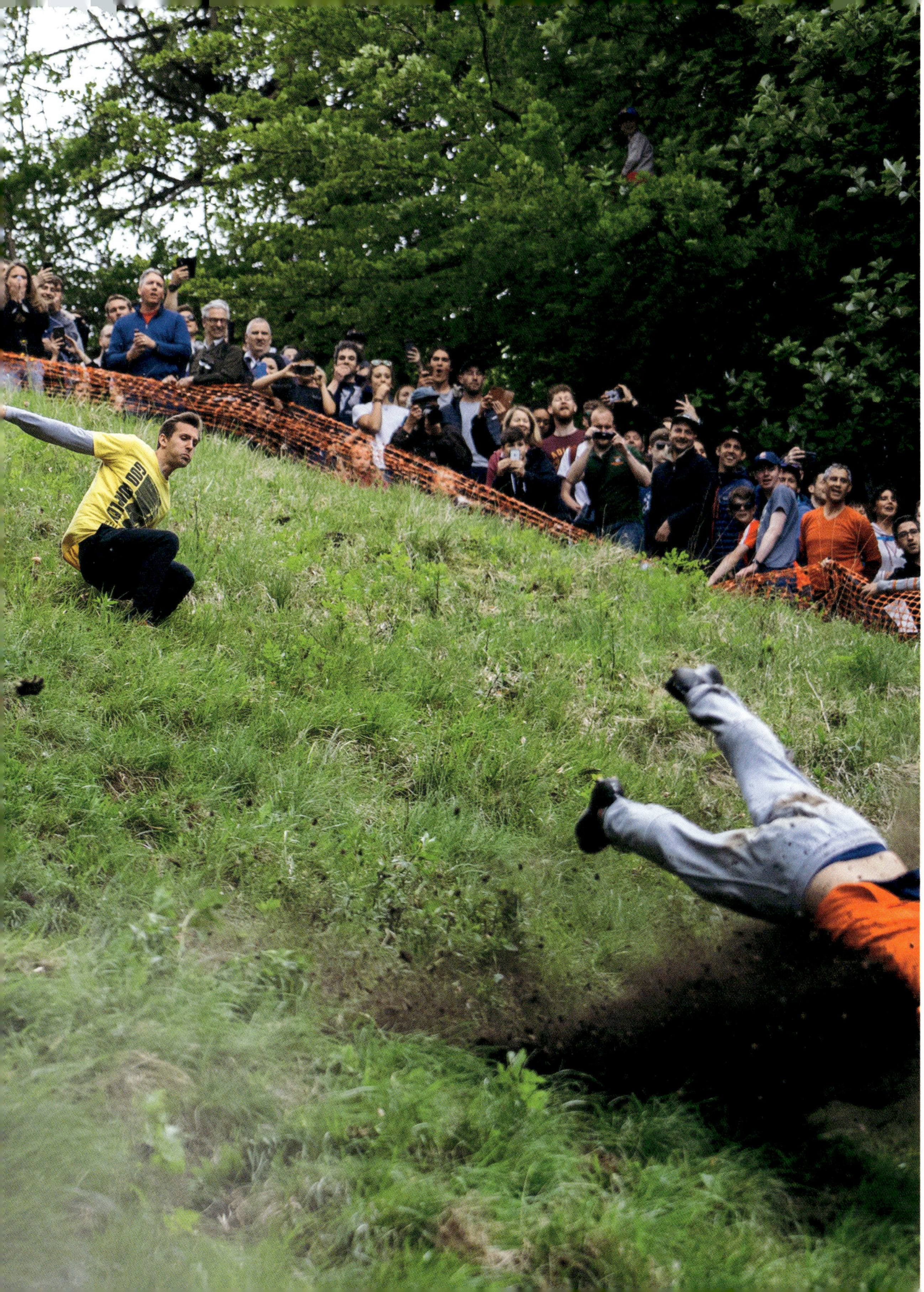

Cheese Rolling

Gloucester, England, UK

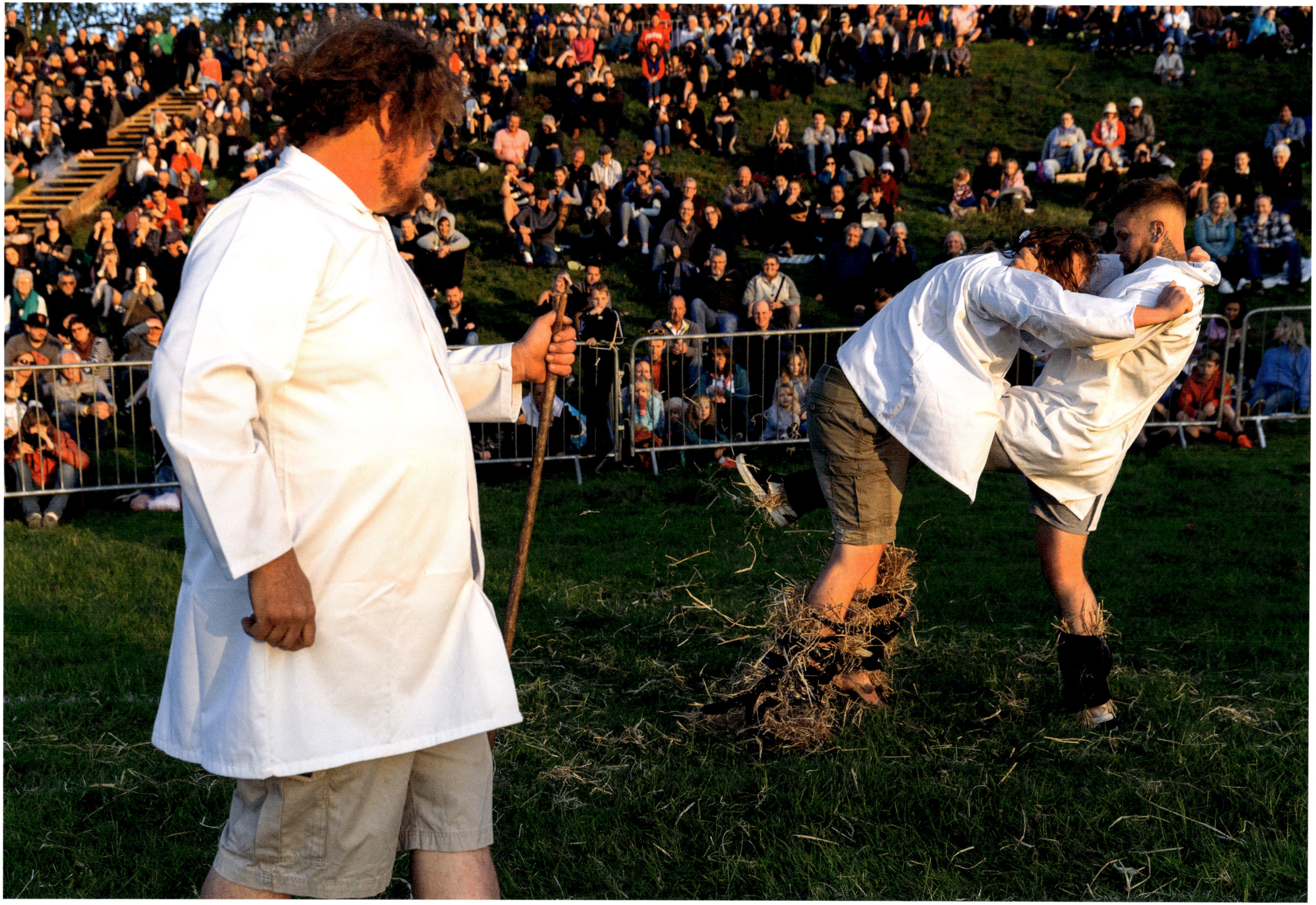

Shin-Kicking World Championships

Chipping Campden, England, UK

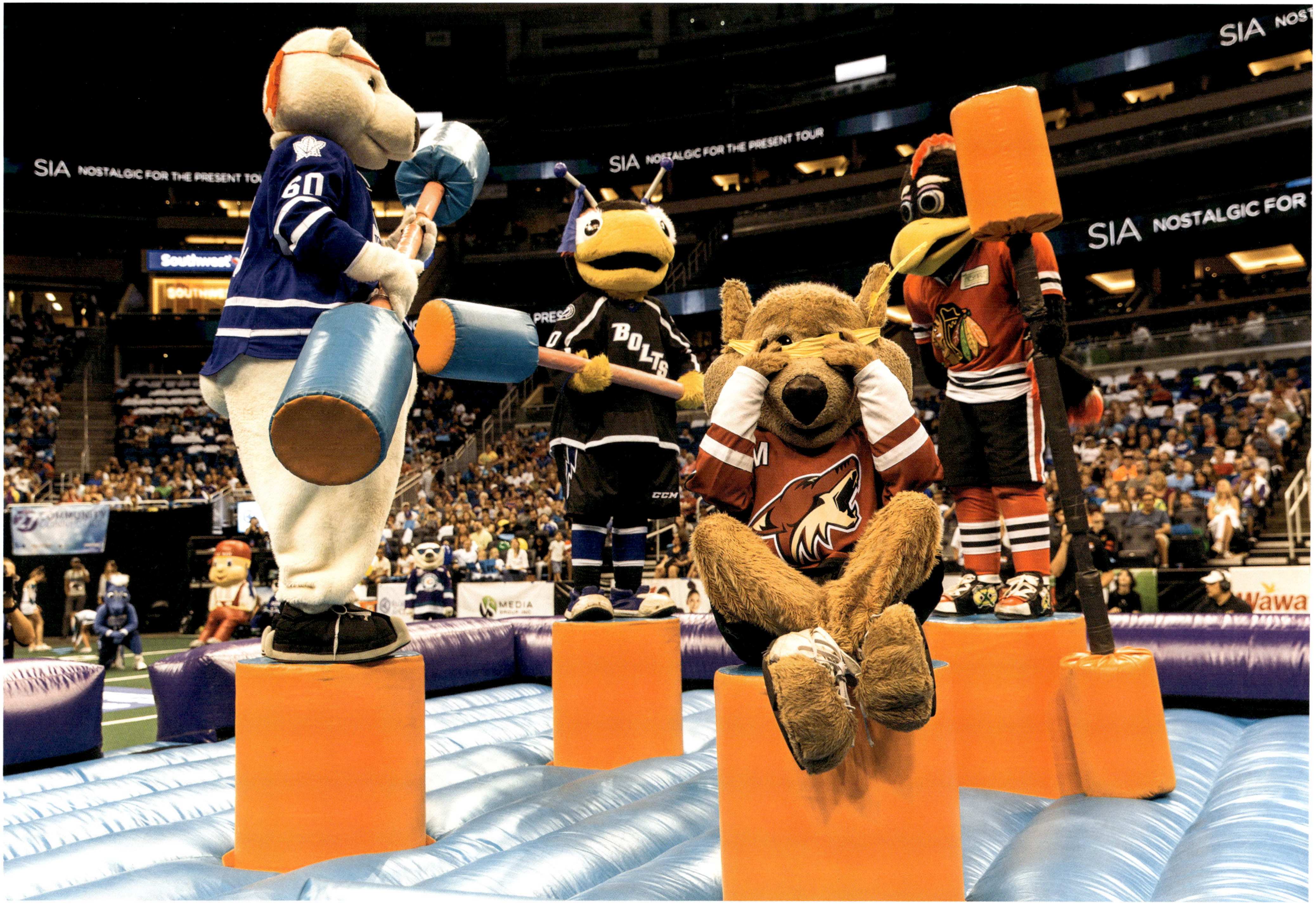

Mascot Games

Orlando, Florida, USA

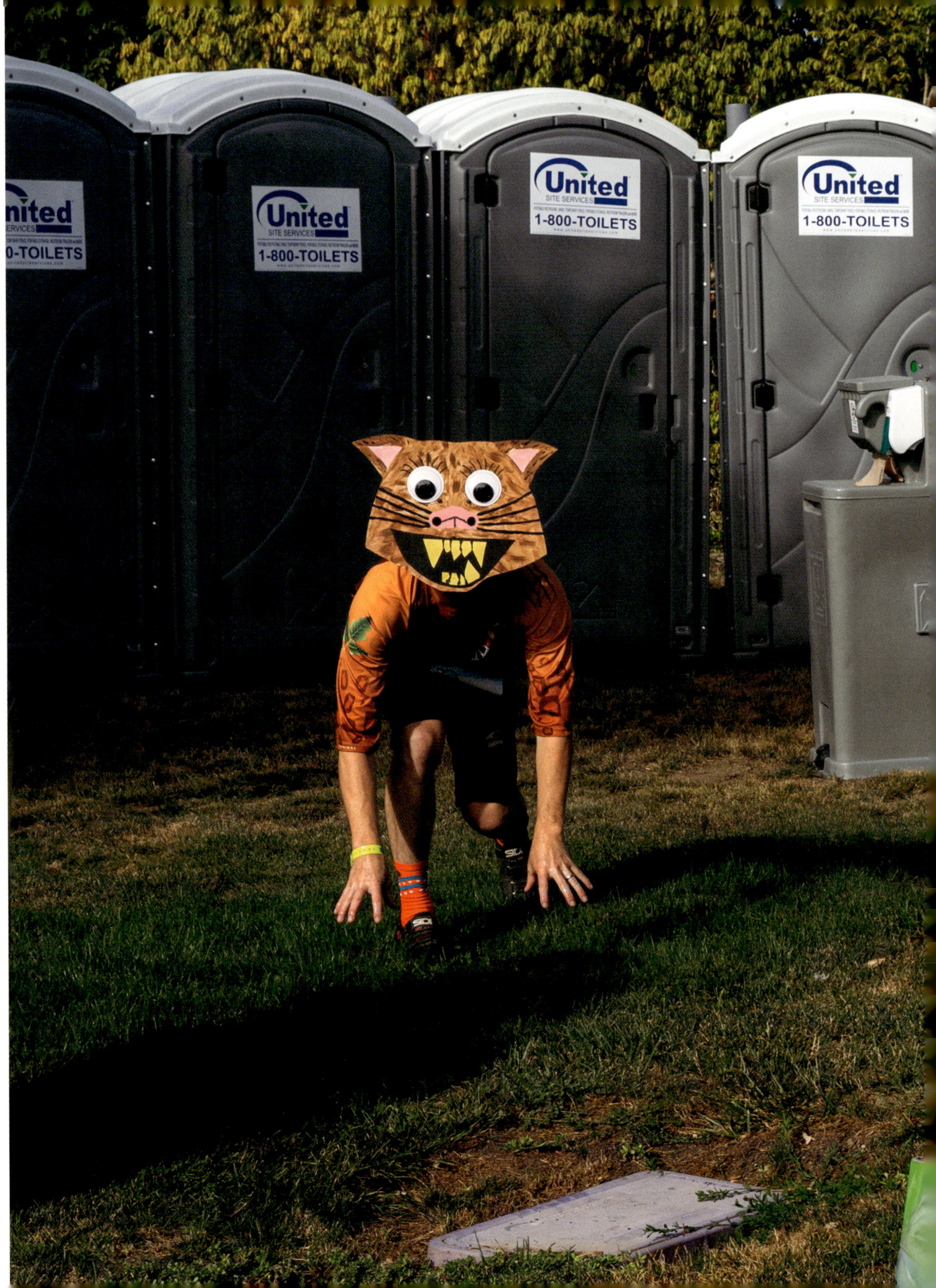

Cyclocross

San Rafael, California, USA

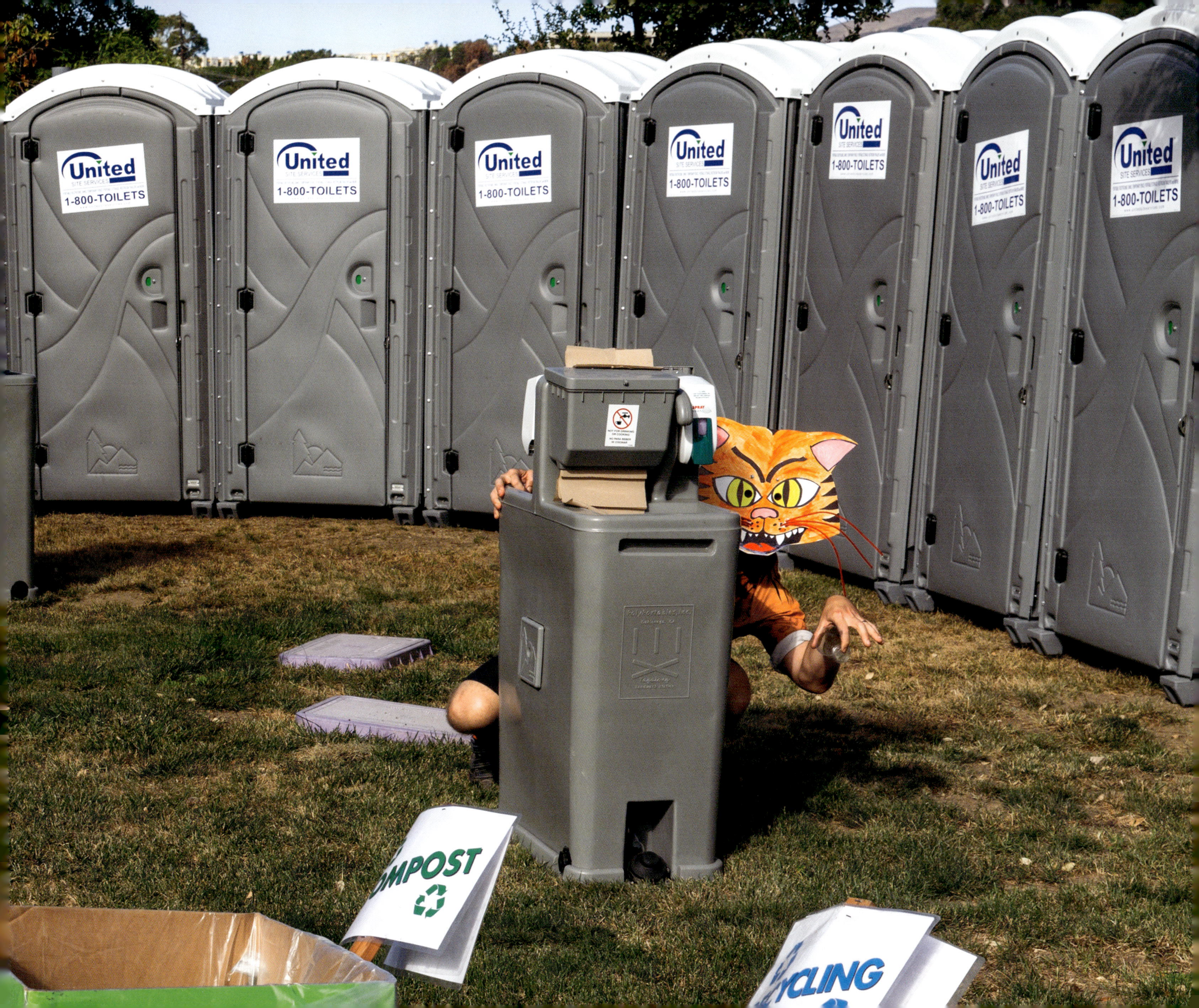
United
1-800-TOILETS
MPOST
YCLING

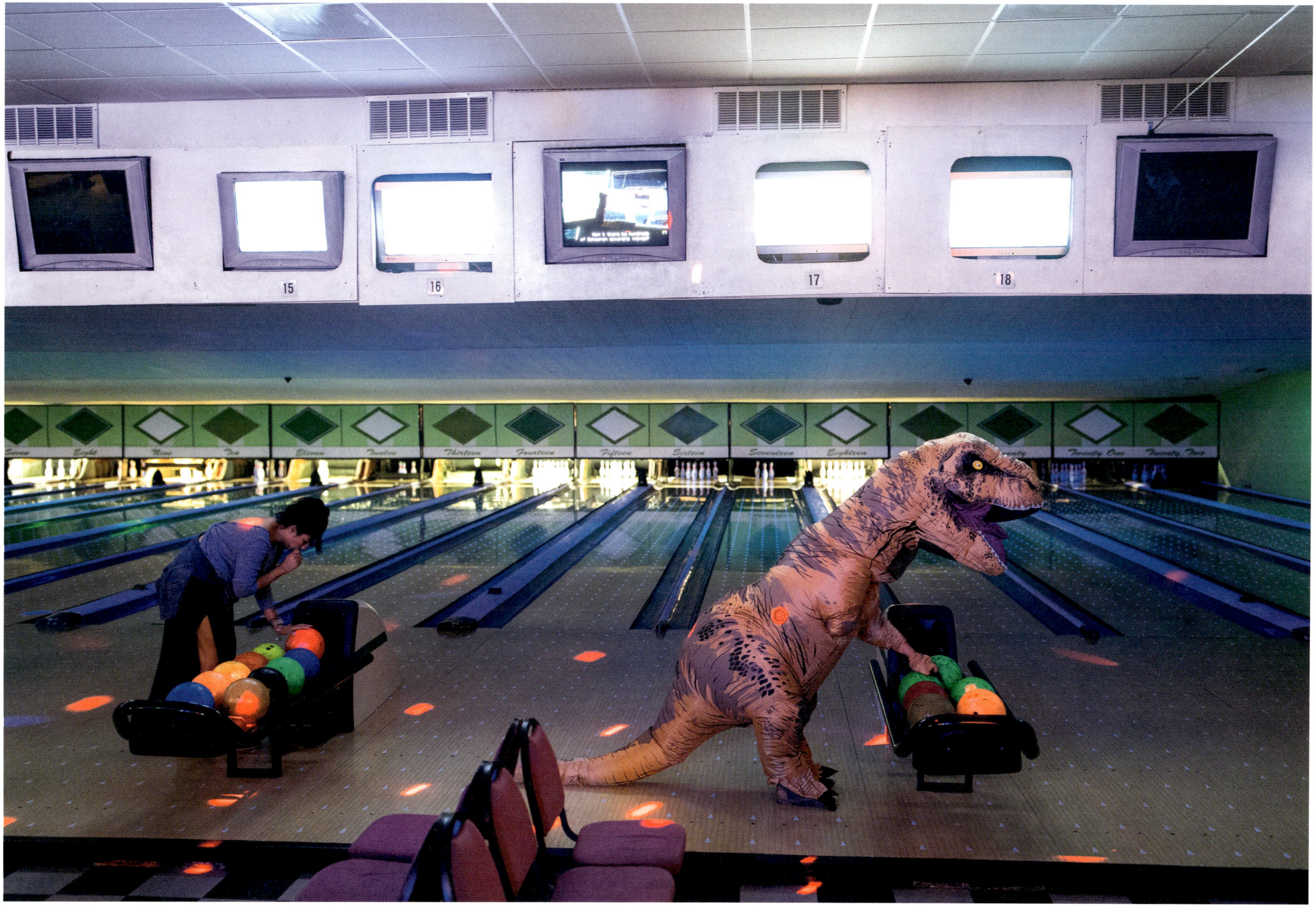

Disco Bowling

Pasadena, California, USA

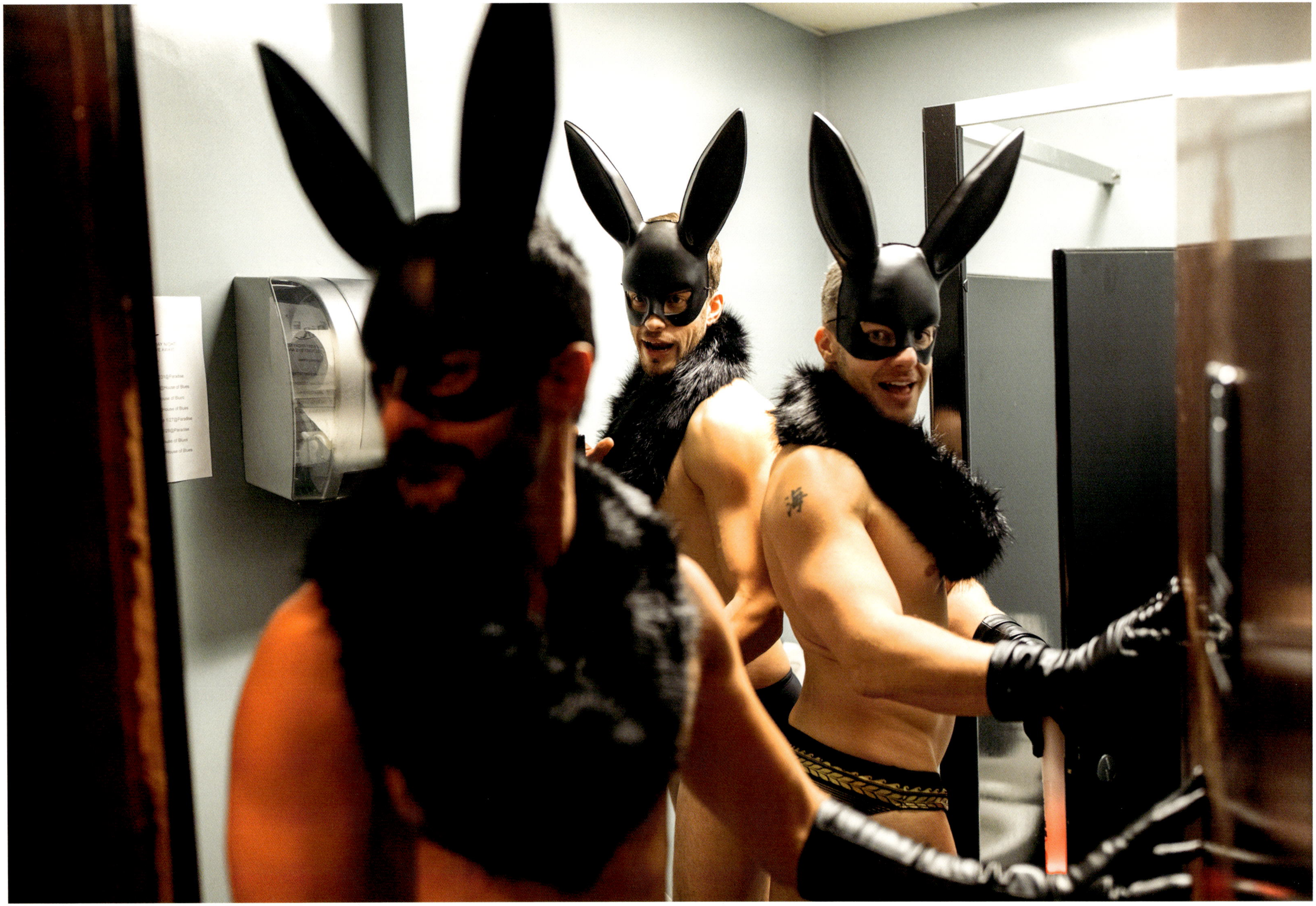

Santa Speedo Run

Boston, Massachusetts, USA

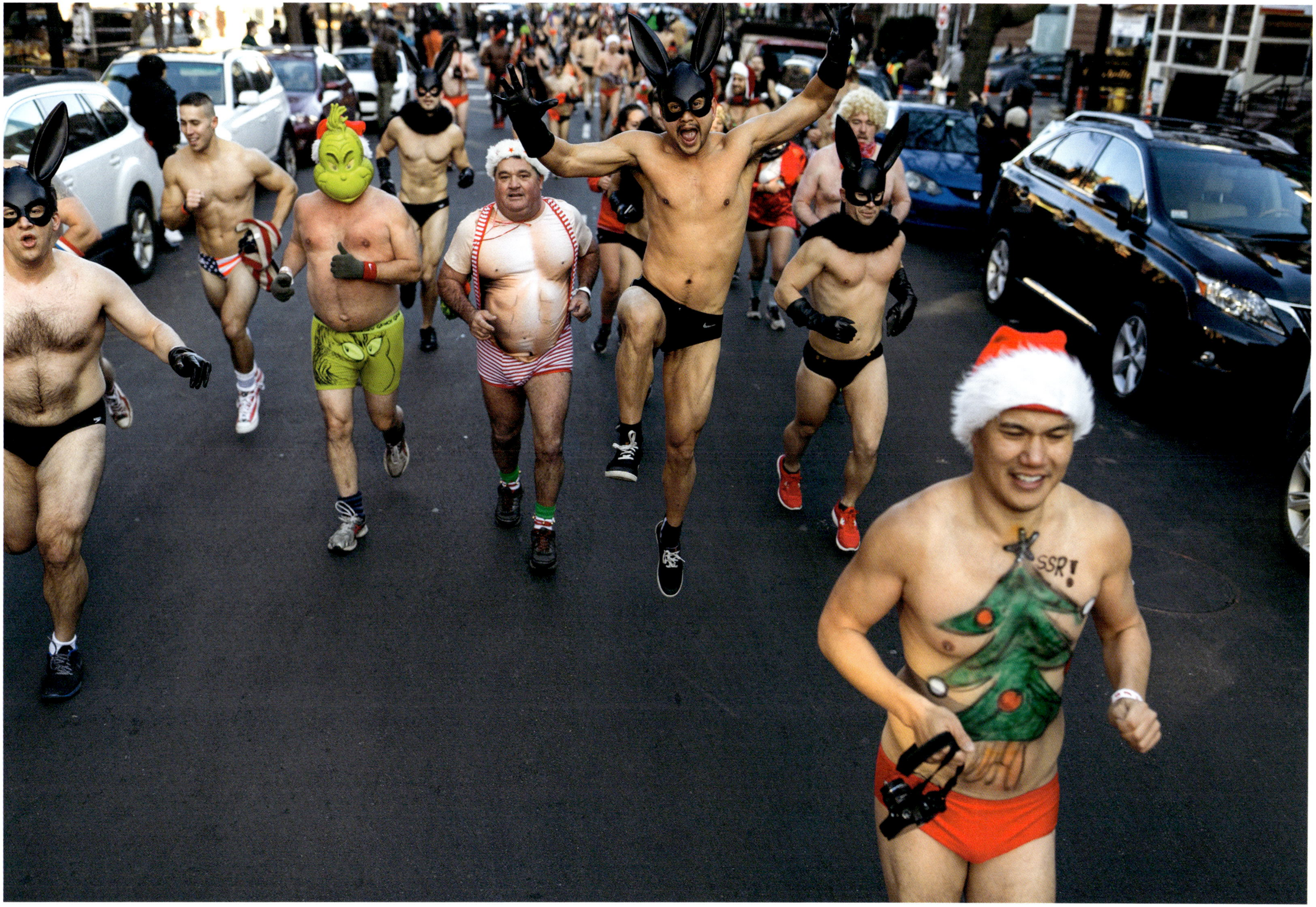

Santa Speedo Run

Boston, Massachusetts, USA

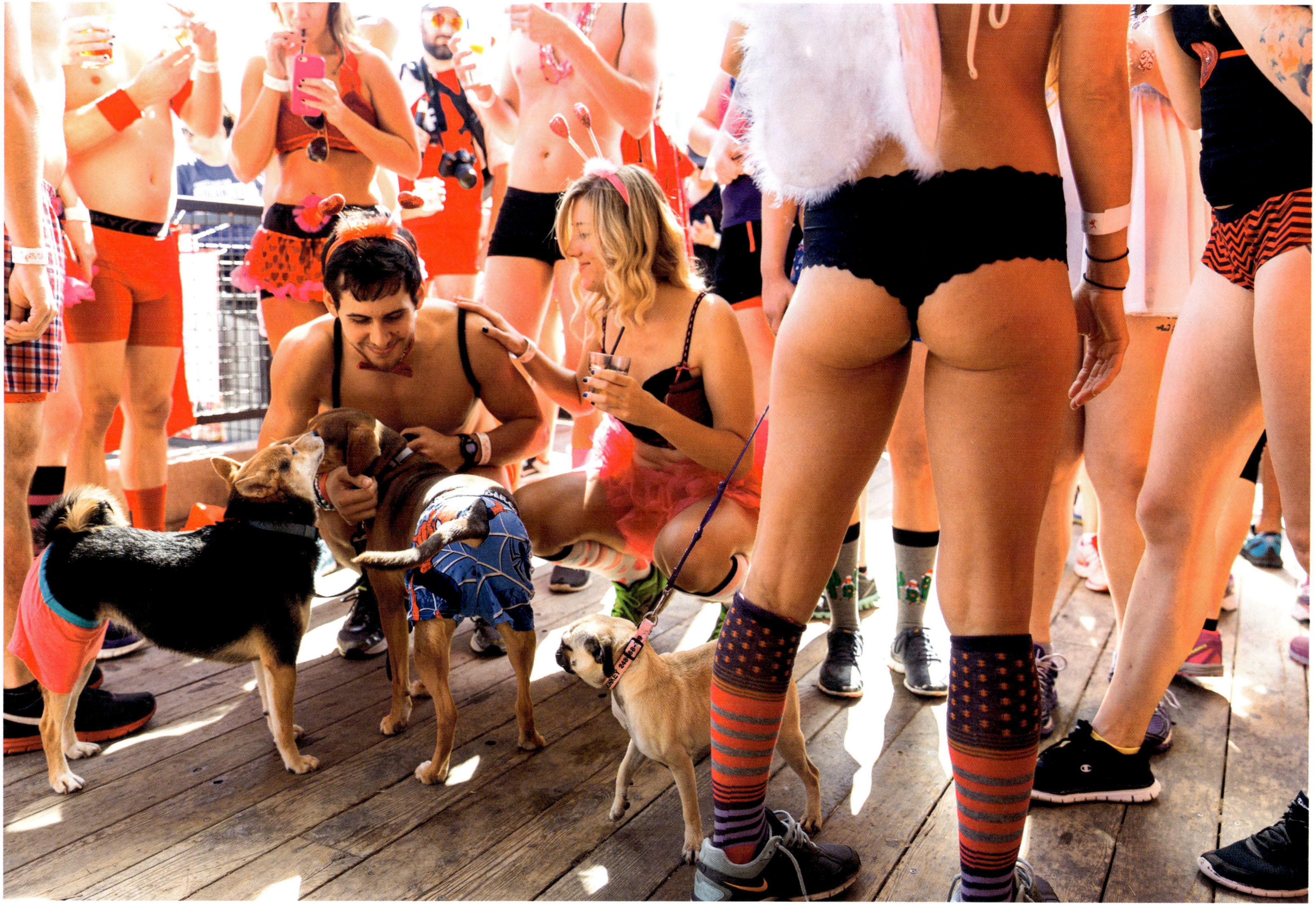

Cupid's Undie Run

Austin, Texas, USA

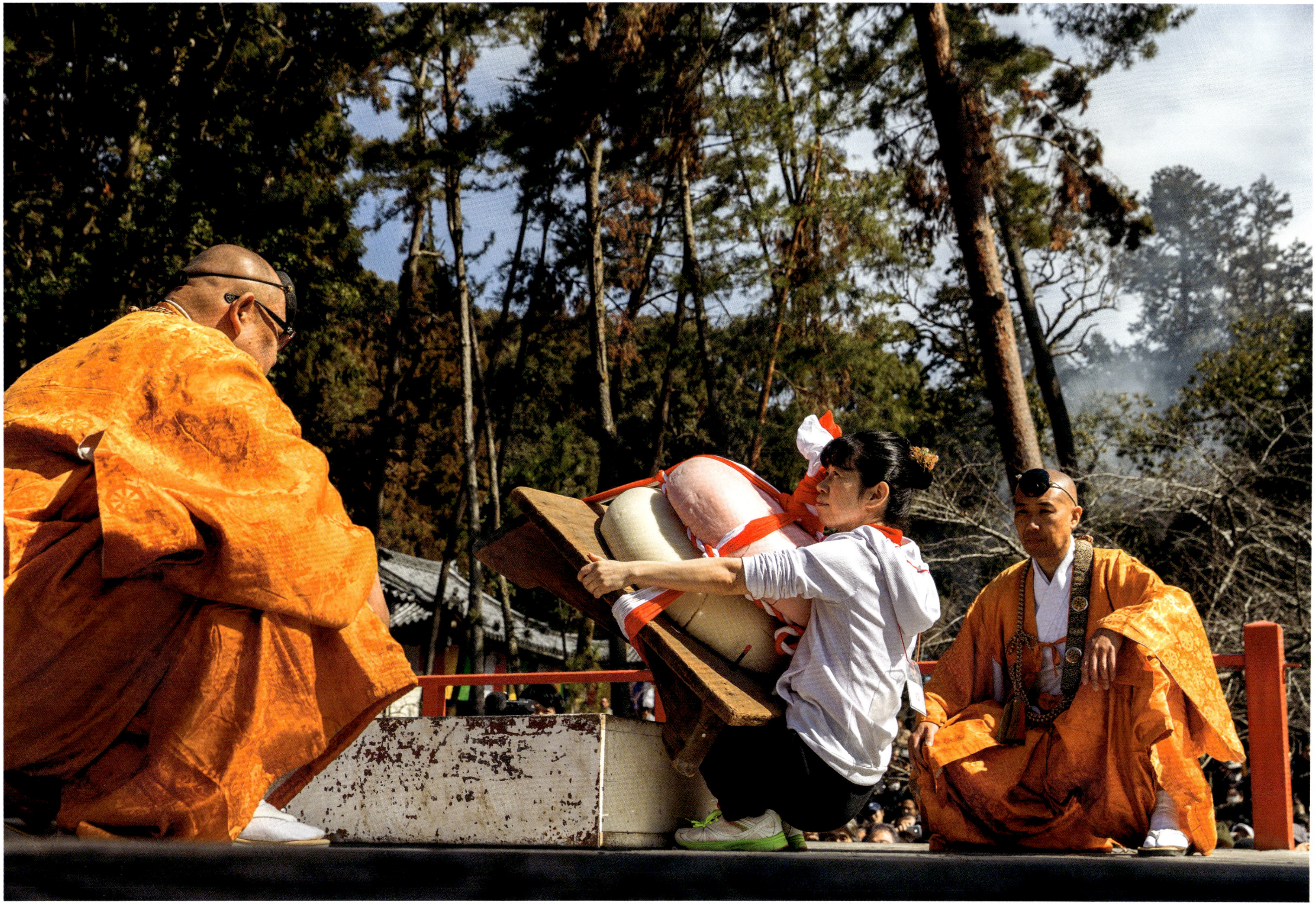

Mochi Lifting

Kyoto, Japan

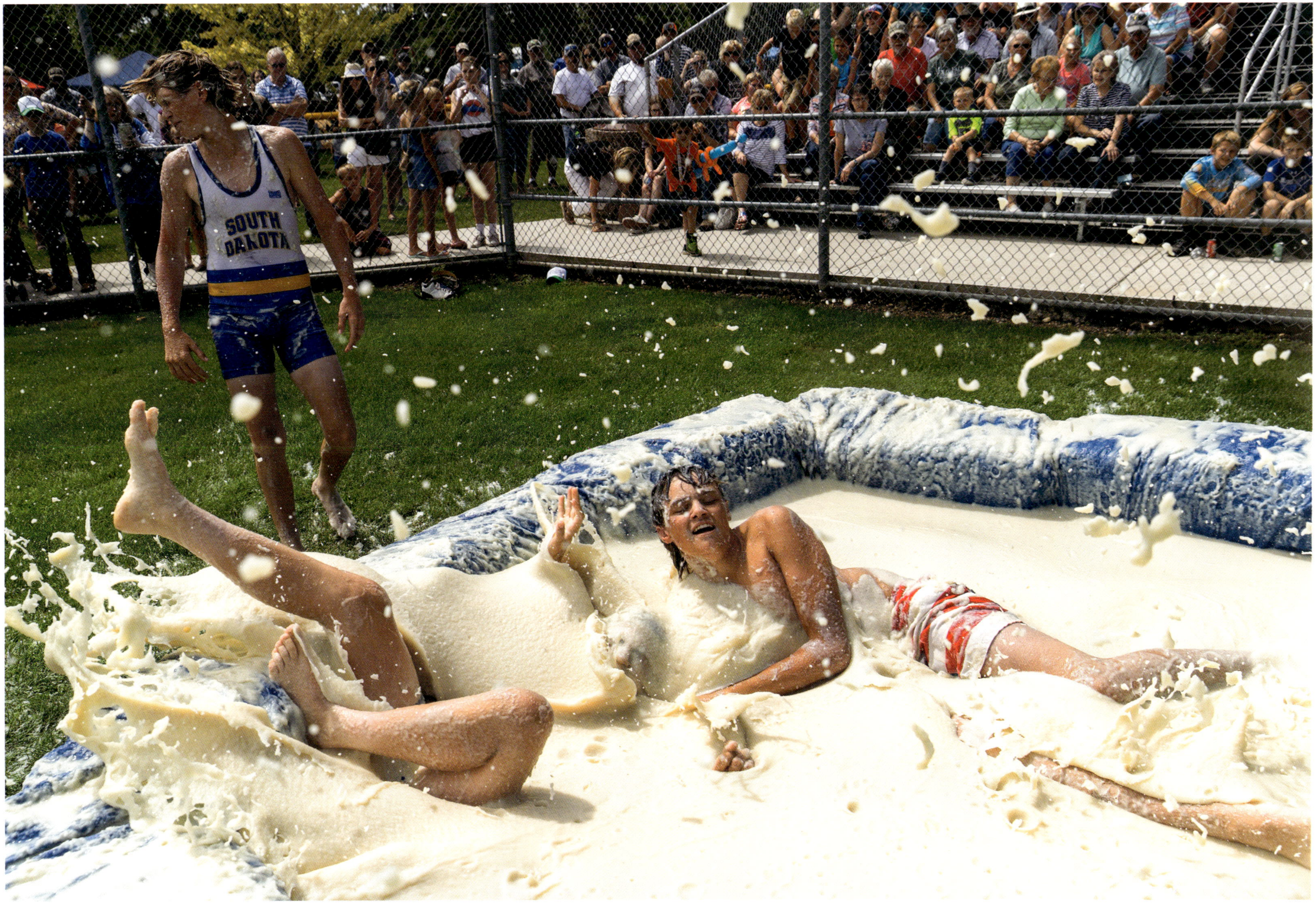

Mashed Potato Wrestling

Clark, South Dakota, USA

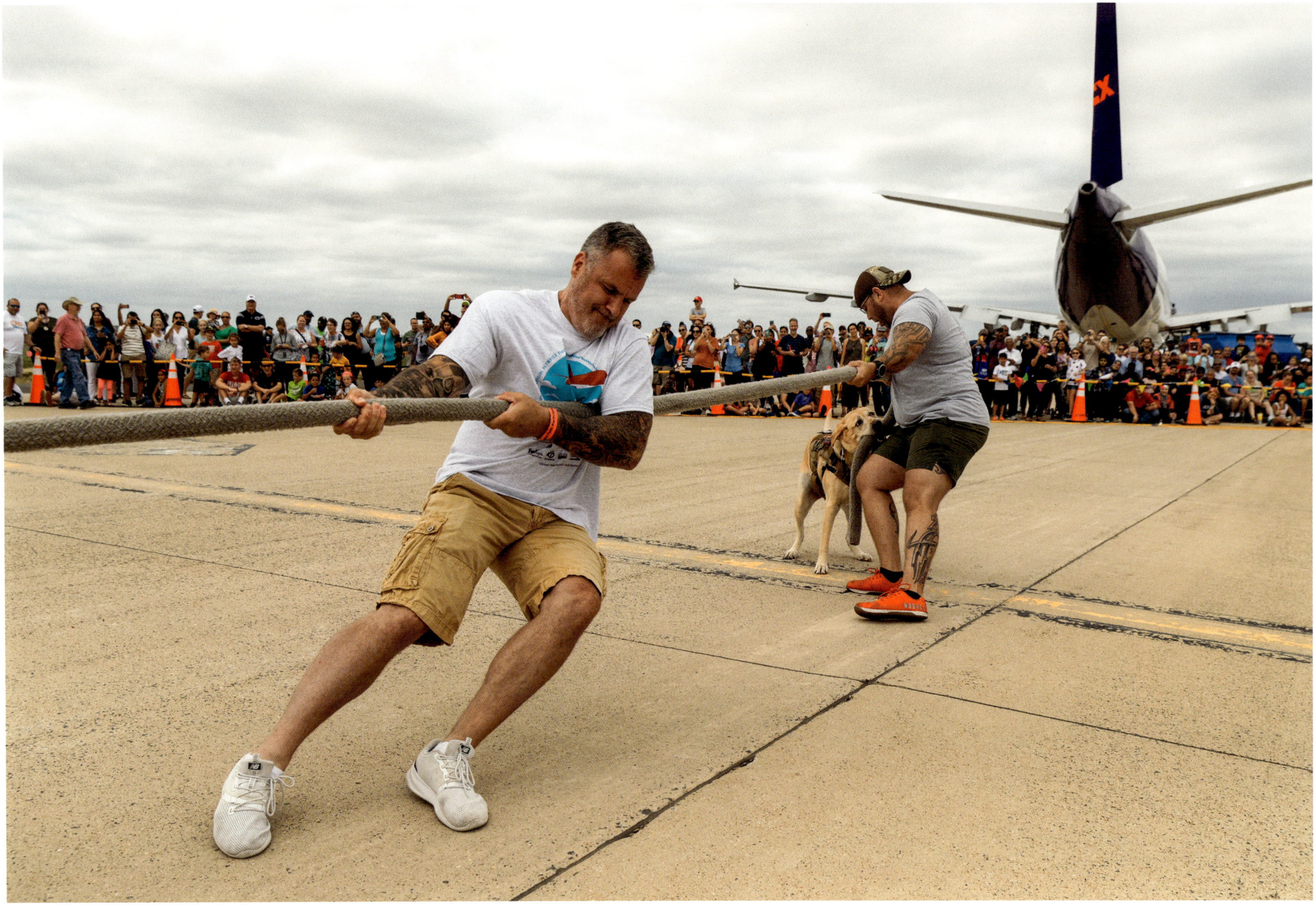

Plane Pull

Dulles, Virginia, USA

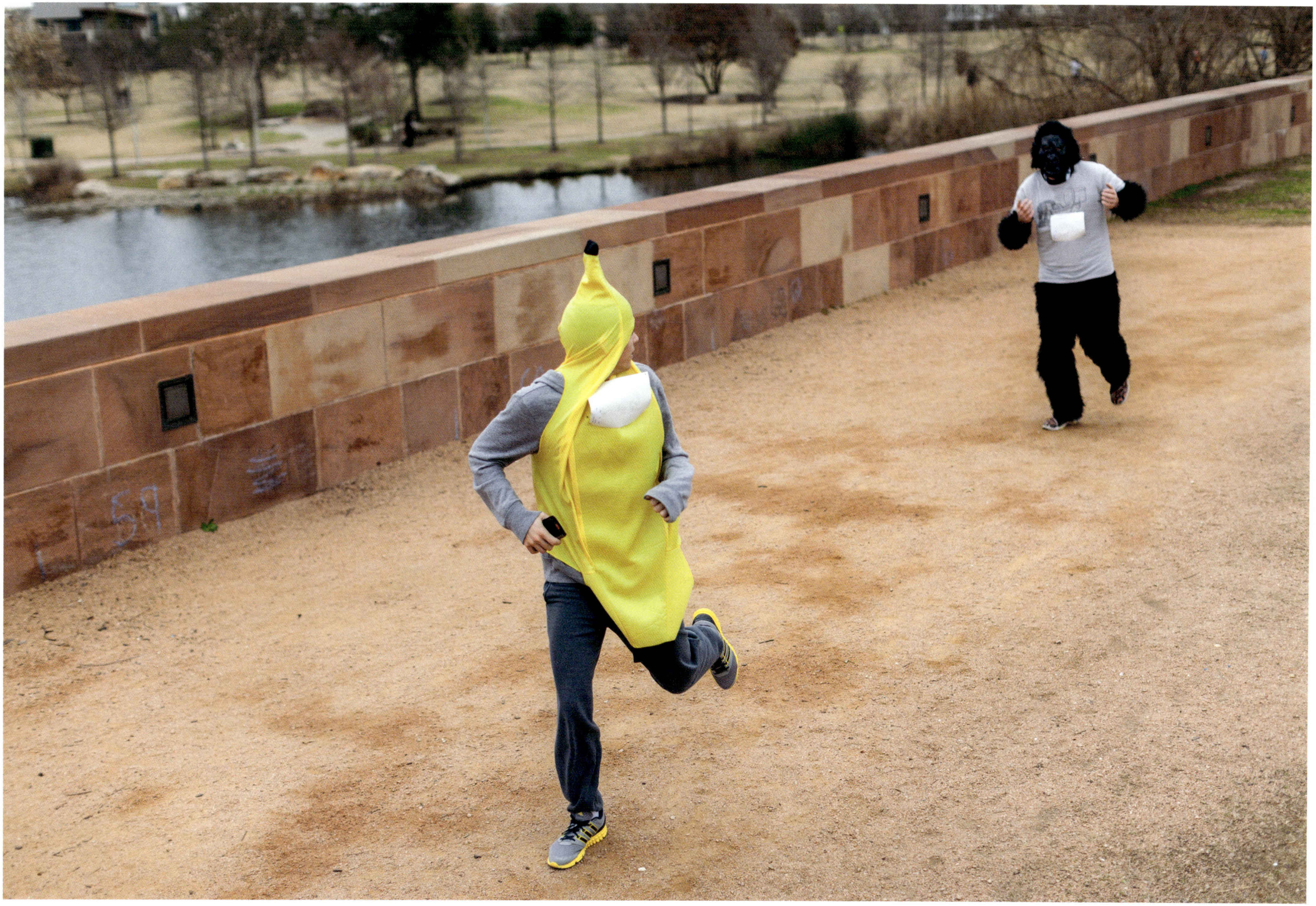

Gorilla Run

Austin, Texas, USA

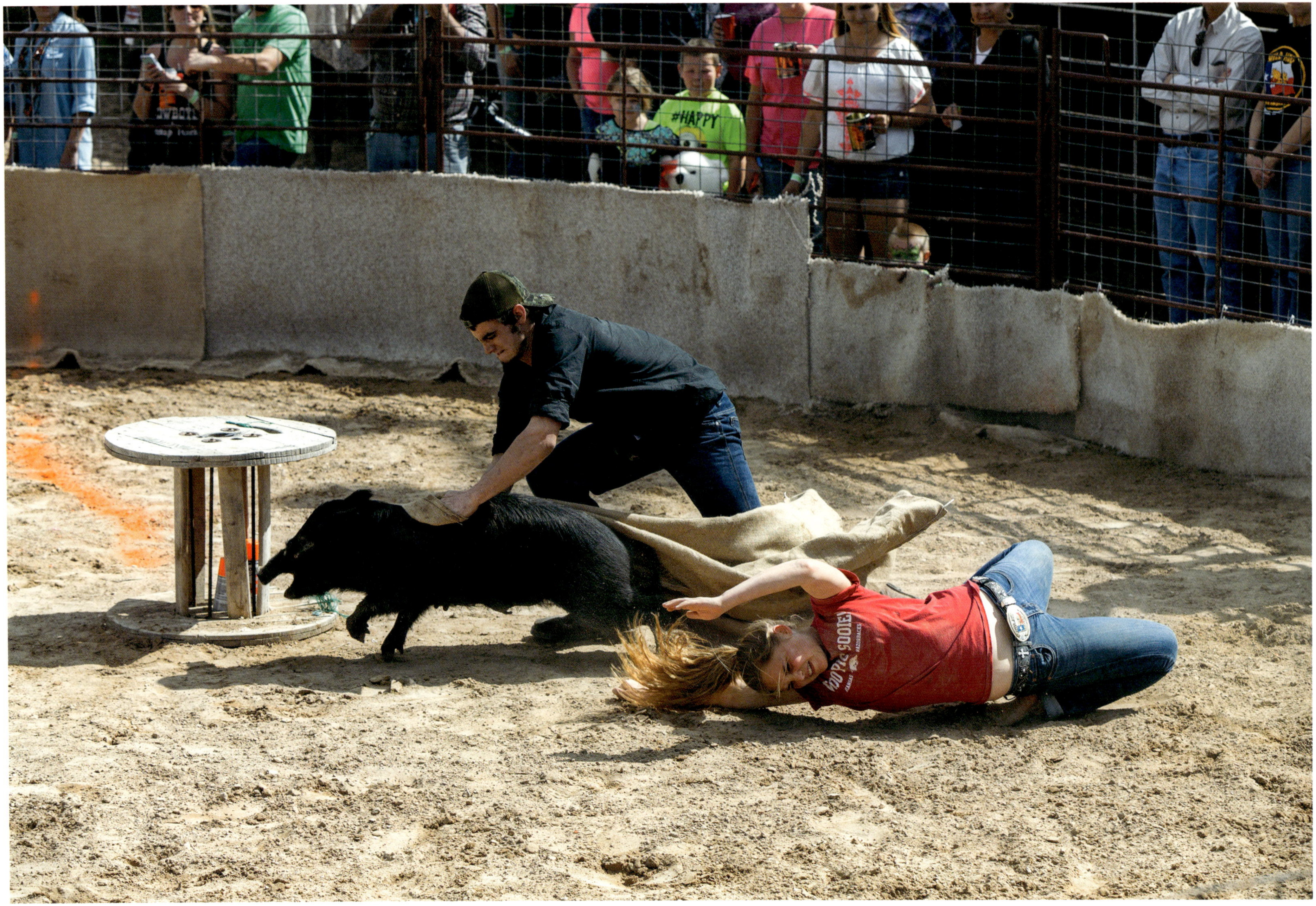

Wild Hog Catch

Bandera, Texas, USA

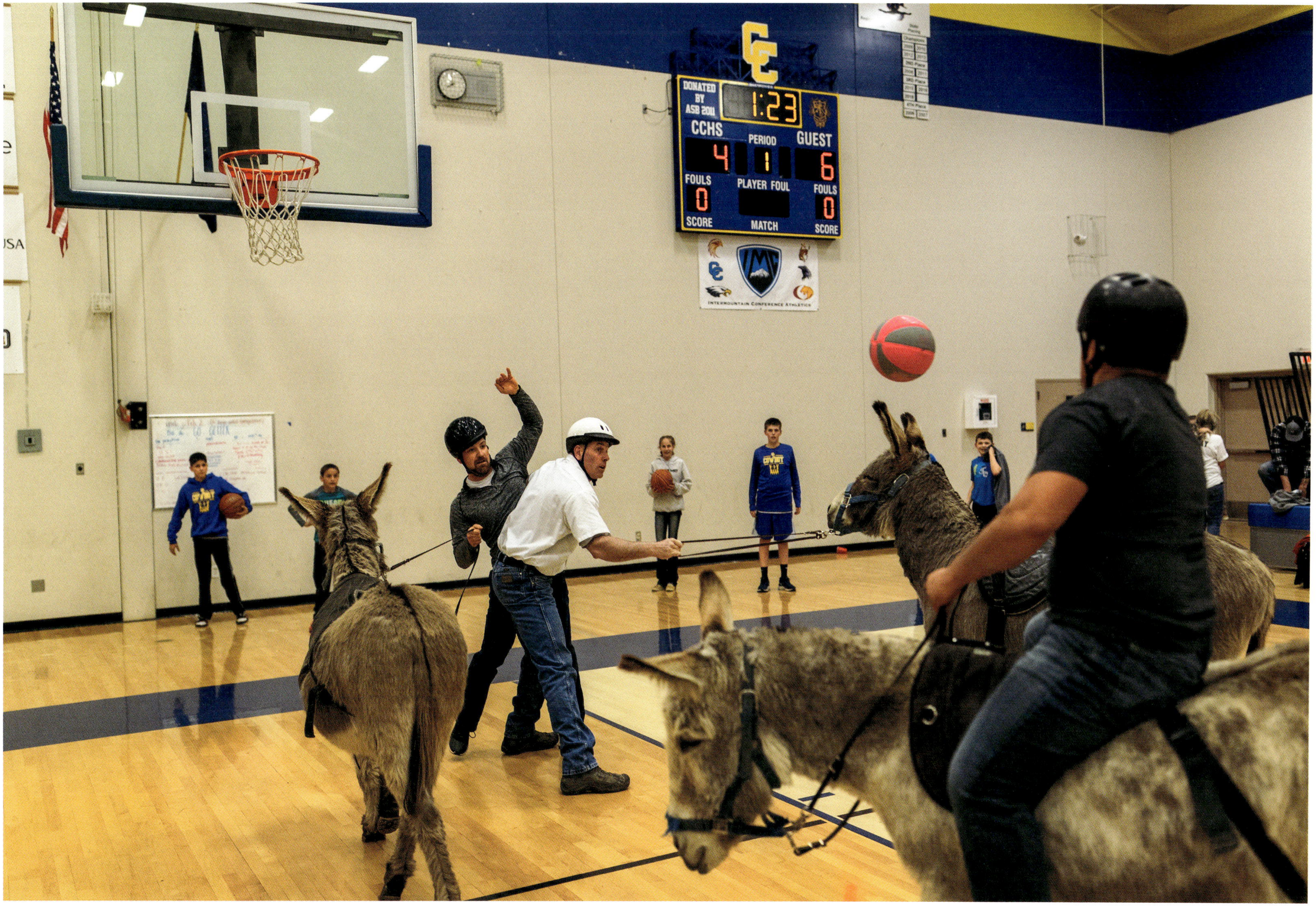

Donkey Basketball

Prineville, Oregon, USA

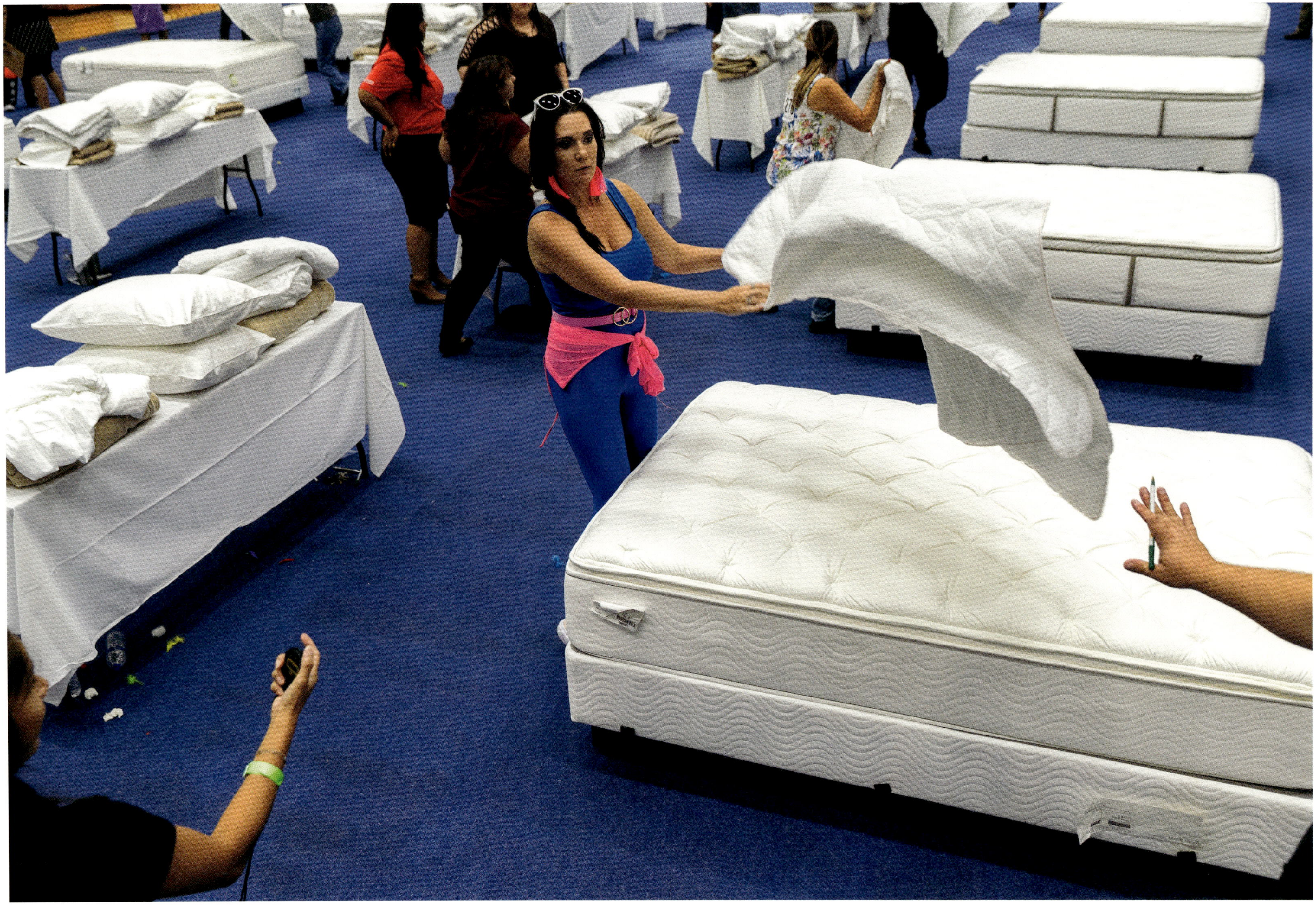

Bed Making Competition

San Antonio, Texas, USA

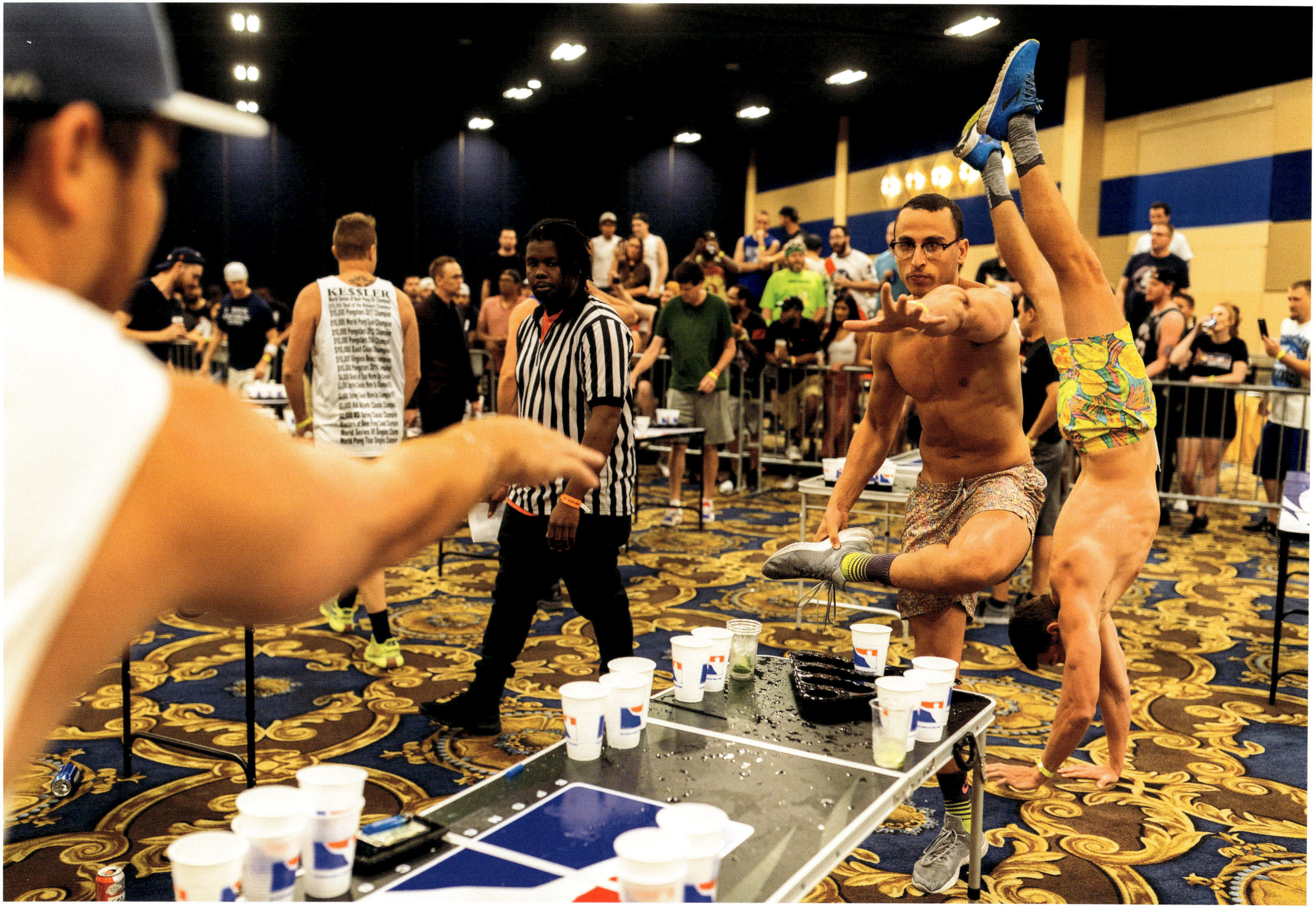

World Series of Beer Pong

Las Vegas, Nevada, USA

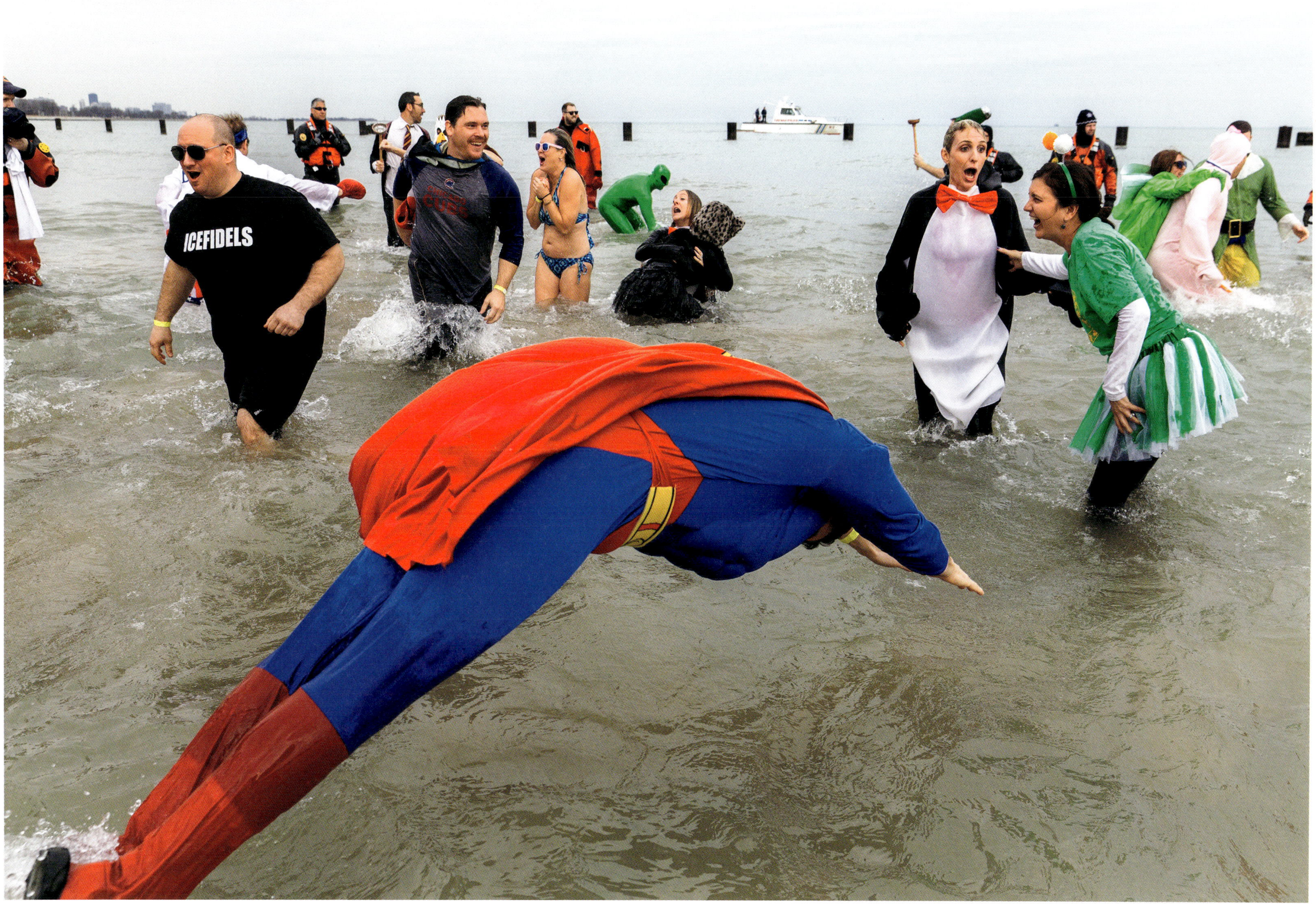

Polar Plunge

Chicago, Illinois, USA

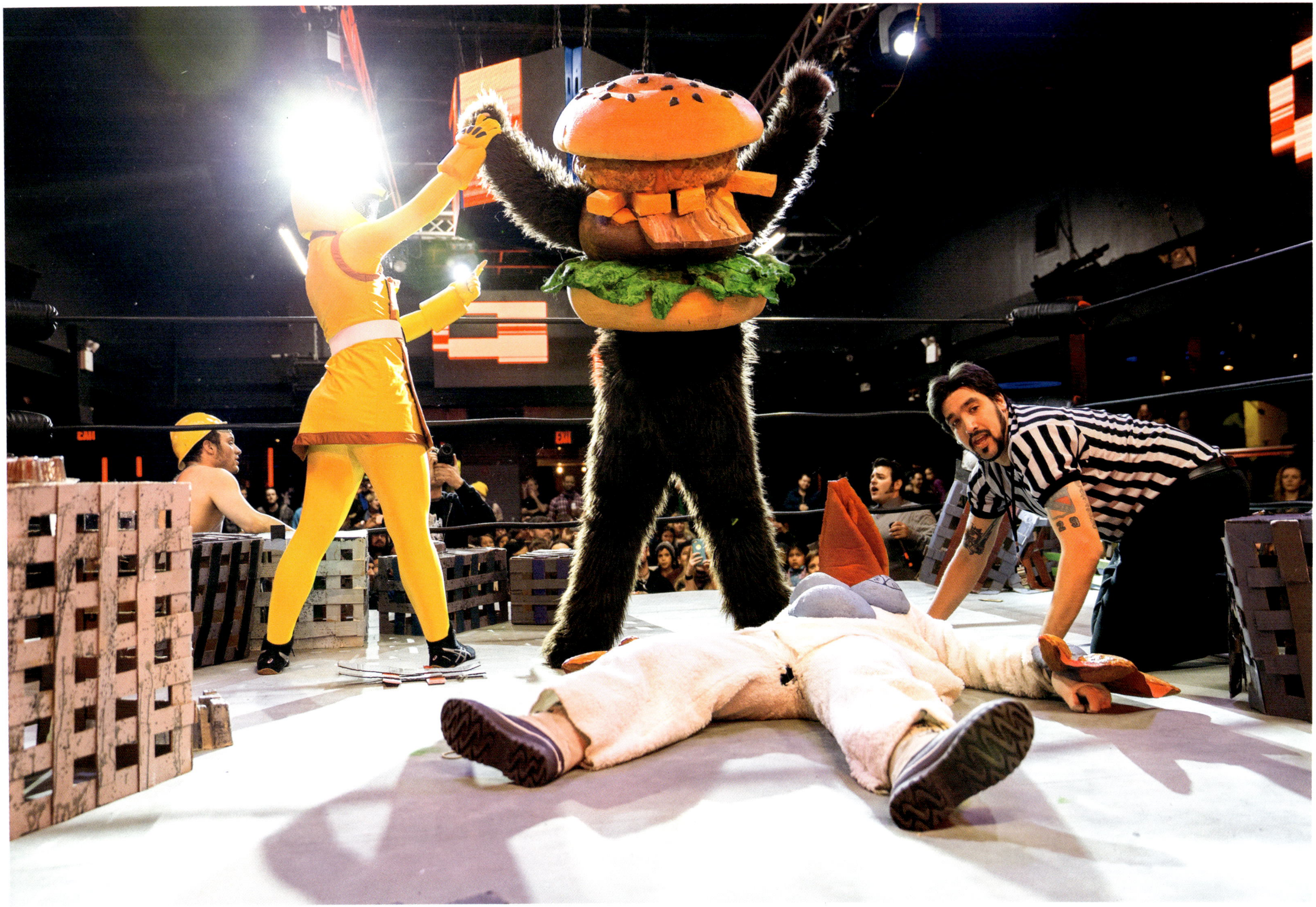

Kaiju Live Monster Wrestling

Queens, New York, USA

The Backword

The day I met Sol Neelman, we were photographing naked men, using painted flaccid penises as foreground elements. We were in an open brick courtyard, and I remember his laugh filling the space and fitting in with the joy of people getting ready to bike naked through the streets of Chicago for the World Naked Bike Ride. John H. White, my Pulitzer Prize-winning photojournalism professor at Columbia College, taught us to be a fly on the wall. My friend Nick Oza, another Pulitzer winner, described himself as a cat, slinking through the house and leaving while everyone wonders where the cat went. Sol doesn't take either approach. He's more like professional wrestling manager Jimmy "The Mouth of the South" Hart—boisterous, bodacious, and bigger than life. He's been that way since Day One.

Whenever Cousin Sol blows into town for a few days (or weeks), life gets better, with more cheese-covered foods, plenty of empty High Life bottles (sometimes on coasters), and hiring the only Pulitzer-winning babysitter I've ever known. The thread that runs through every experience with Sol is finding joy every day. Even getting children to eat their vegetables becomes a game show with Cousin Sol, who gleefully tells them to "EAT. YOUR. PEEEEEEEEEEAS." Very few people give you space, and encouragement, to be exactly what you want and to make sure you're having fun doing it.

Looking at the wonderful photos in *More Weird Sports*, it's hard to know who's having more fun—Sol, or the people he's photographing. While attending the Redneck Fishing Tournament with Sol a few years ago, our boats passed each other and Sol was holding his broken camera overhead like it was the Stanley Cup. A 10-pound fish had jumped out of the water, slammed into him and snapped the lens off, doing hundreds of dollars of damage. Yet hours later we're smiling, arm in arm with a man in a thong who just won the "tighty-whitey" contest. (He defeated his own son.) It was unforgettable, and so very Sol. A few months later, Cousin Sol and I were in Maine for the U.S. National Toboggan Championships. We were flying down a chute flat on our backs going 40 mph in freezing temperatures, with his head stuck in my crotch as he's screaming, "What is happening? Whooooooooo!" That scene actually appeared in a TV commercial. We are so goddamn lucky.

Every picture in *More Weird Sports* captures a moment like that. They tell stories of joy (and more than a little booze, sweat, and costumes.) Whenever Sol talks to my photojournalism classes, he talks more about who he was with when he took his photos than how he photographed them: I was at Flaming Tetherball with Erika or I went to Llama Races with Barker or I watched Bog Snorkeling with Liz. And that, at heart, is what Weird Sports is all about: the joy of sharing what you love with others.

Years ago, as Sol was sleeping on the floor of my living room after some kid's or adult's birthday celebration, my mother said, "It's nice to finally have a world-famous photographer in the house." It is, mom. The house, and my life, is a more joyful place with Sol in it.

Cousin Rob Hart
Honky-tonk redneck fisherman,
veteran vegetarian, and his mother's
second favorite photographer

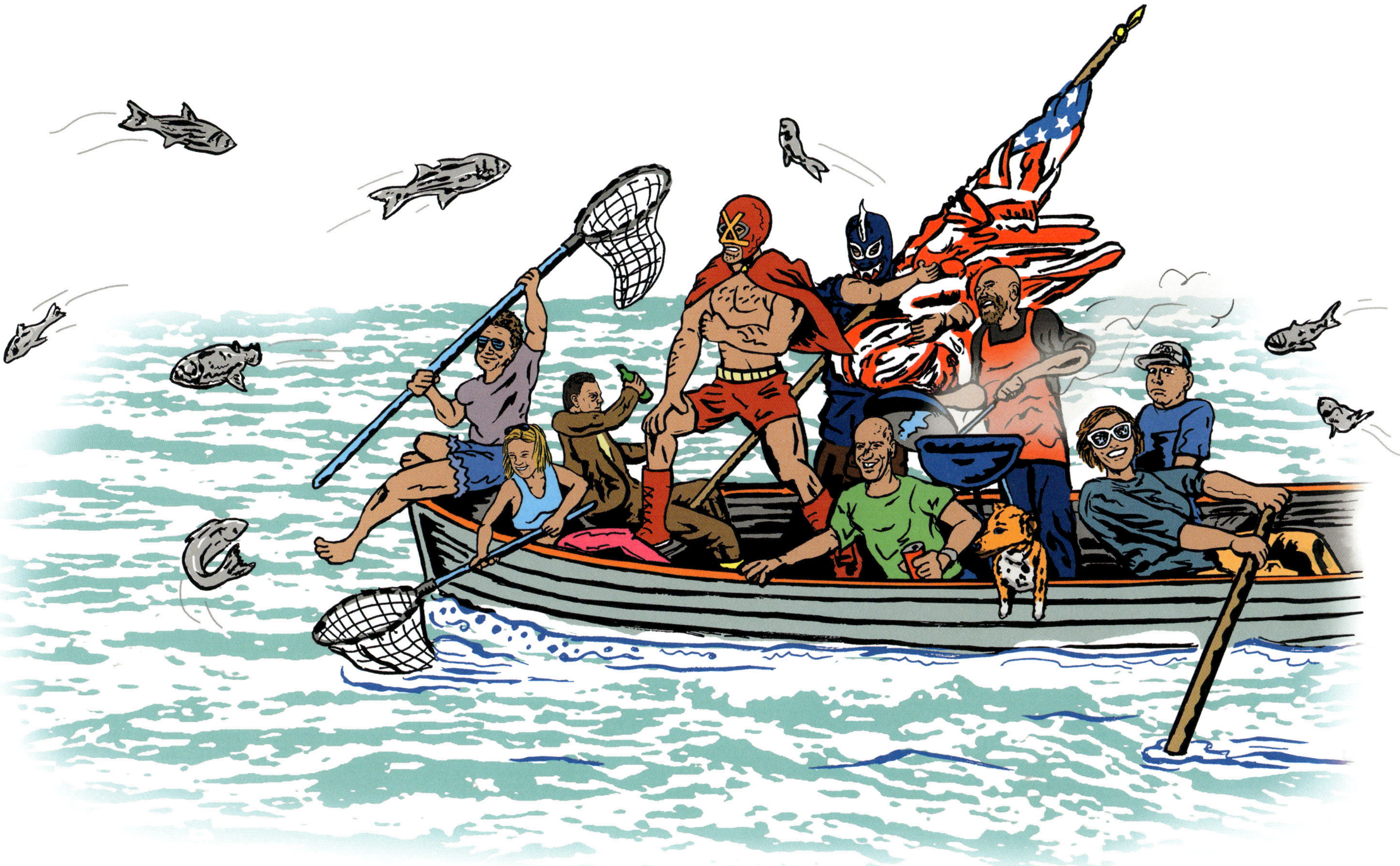

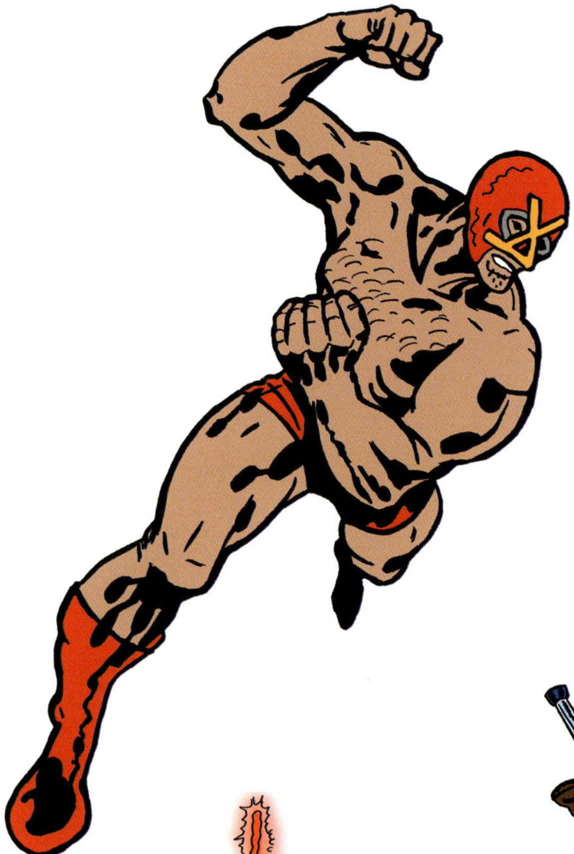

The Final Frontier

Joy: the final frontier. These are the voyages of a Weird Sports aficionado. His continuing mission: to explore strange recreation. To seek out peculiar pastimes and eccentric endeavors. To boldly photograph activities no photographer has photographed before!

Geeky way to start this? Absolutely. But the Trekkie in me loves it. And it totally fits. As a kid growing up in the '70s, I sat entirely too close to our black-and-white TV, religiously following the exploits of Captain James T. Kirk and continually disappointed that there weren't ever any new episodes. (I didn't get the memo that the original *Star Trek* series ended before I was born.)

What fascinated me most as a kiddo cadet was joining the crew of the USS Enterprise as it discovered strange worlds that seemed like home, just a wee bit different. In one dark yet fascinating episode, Kirk and Co. visit a planet exactly like earth, ruled by children. What a wild idea!

That pretty much sums up Weird Sports: A world inhabited by (adult-aged) children racing downhill in Barbie Jeeps, sprinting uphill on stilts through the streets of an Italian village, or crashing through a wall of beer cans while riding a motorcycle at Sturgis. Residents of this magical realm often wear costumes—although a few wear only their birthday suits—and are usually seen with a cold one in hand, laughing with friends, and wondering why more people aren't in on the fun.

And just as the creators of *Star Trek* reimagined the familiar to create something wonderful, so too

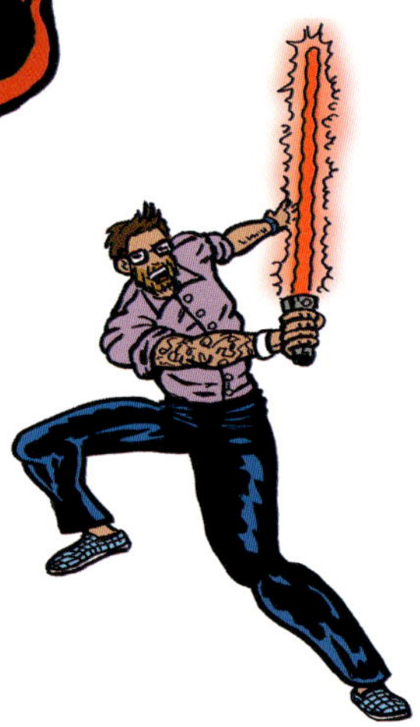

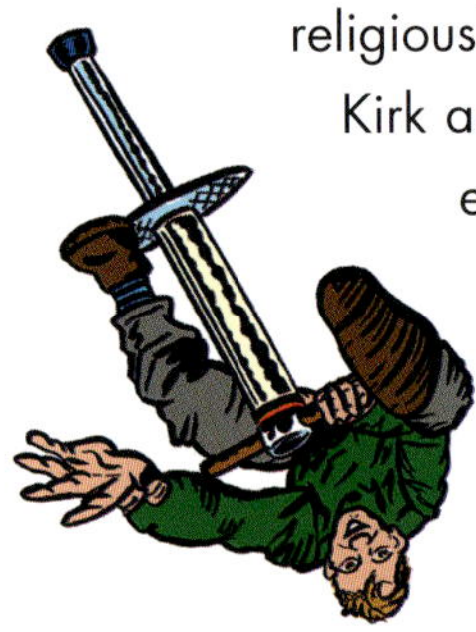

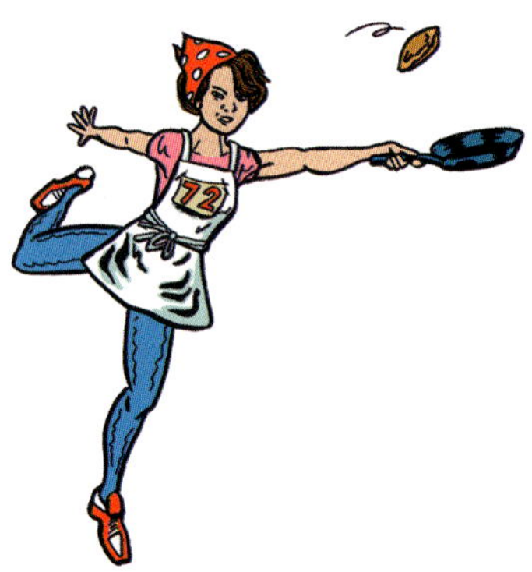

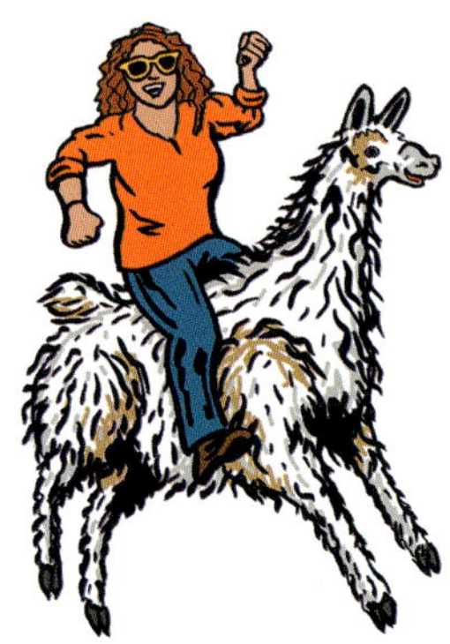

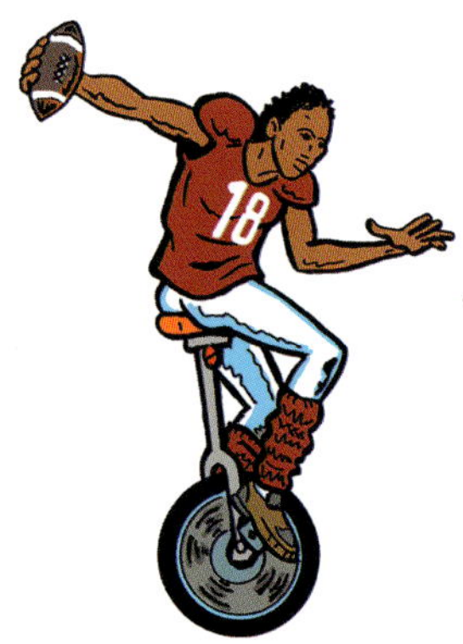

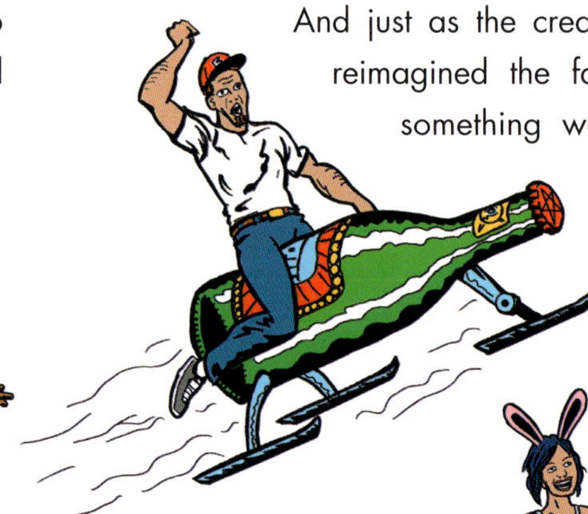

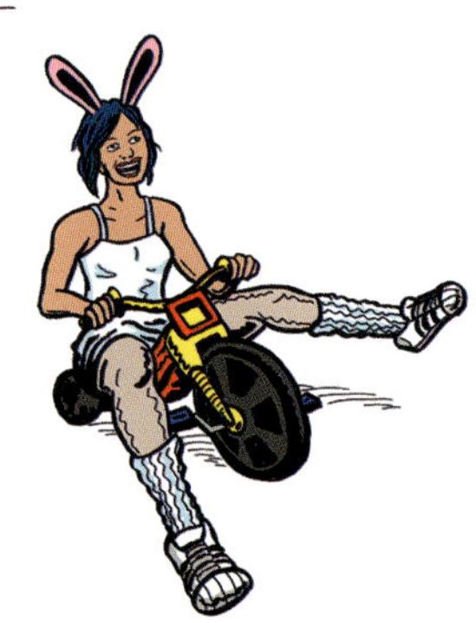

do the creators of Weird Sports. They'll hold a wrestling match, but have contestants compete in a kiddie pool of mashed potatoes. Or require them to deadlift 100 pounds of mochi. Or race around a track in a Model T with a pig under an arm.

You get the idea: Have fun. Find your joy. Grab a tallboy and share some laughs with friends.

I was truly fortunate to stumble upon this world more than 15 years ago, when I found a way to combine my love of sports, travel, and weird shit. My journey has often seemed to spiral wildly out of control, but looking back on it now, I realize that I was always on course, always exactly where I was supposed to be. After photographing more than 200 events on five continents, I've made a lot of friends, shared a lot of laughs and, yes, drunk a lot of pivo. (See a pattern?)

Not bad for a kid who spent his childhood looking for a bit of fun and a sense of connection.

What you hold in your hands is a photographic time capsule, a look back at some of the weirdest, most joyful moments from a trip that's gone on far longer than I ever expected. The final addition to this book, from an amazingly athletic beer drinking contest called Gelände Quaffing, was taken on March 11, 2020. It's a surreal memento from the final day of the before times.

A lot has changed since then. But one thing that hasn't is the universal desire to feel seen and heard. We all crave acceptance and understanding. We all want to express our joy, have fun, and find our community. And that, at heart, is what Weird Sports—the events, and the book trilogy—is all about.

When I look through my Weird Sports photos, my first thoughts are usually about the friends who joined me at each event. Barker at Mashed Potato Wrestling, Melissa at Barbie Jeep Racing, Cousin Rob at Redneck Fishing, Jules at Chuckwagon Racing, James at the Angola Prison Rodeo, Dustin at Pogopalooza. I set out all those years ago to photograph communities having fun, never realizing that the fun would include people so close to me.

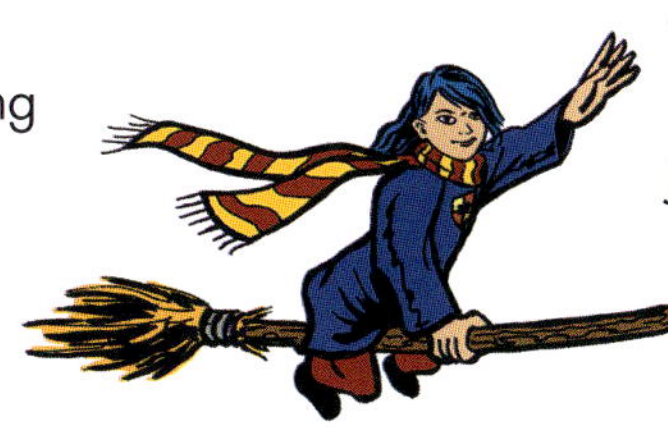

Discovering Weird Sports has been one of the greatest gifts of my life. Not only did it give me purpose professionally, it allowed me to reconnect with old friends and meet new ones. It has provided immeasurable joy and an ever-growing community.

After all, happiness and connection is what life's all about. Go out there and find yours.

Live long and prosper, weirdos.

Sol Neelman
Failed pro wrestler turned sports photographer and seeker of connection and joy

Sol

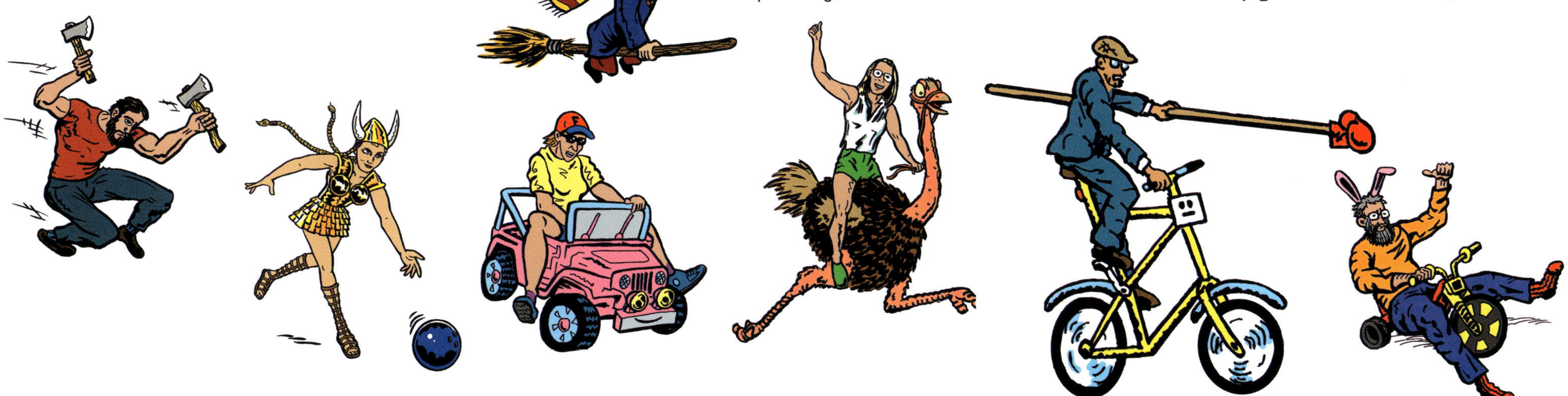

The Thank Yous

My career and life has never gone as I imagined, but it has usually exceeded expectations. And it's in large part because of the love and support of my community. As I like to say, it takes a village to raise a Weird Sports photographer. I'm about to thank everyone on planet earth—and their pet. So grab a salty snack, cold suds and sit back. In a weird alphabetic order that will only make sense to me, I'd like to spotlight these wonderful humans for their energy, love, and support:

The inspirational community of aphotoaday.org, Ahmet, Shelley & Aaron, Berner, The Becker family, Alexis, Amy Rose, The VanderZandens, Andy, Arianna, Pants & Noles, La familia Gutierrez, R2R & Matt, Branndon, Carolyn & Ray, Chip, Pietsch, Colin and Matt, Cooper, Dale Smith, Kiwis Leah, Susan, Dan & Dani, Darryl, Amanda & Ada, eh, Deb & Mike, The Detricks, Dustins Drankoski and Franz, Emily, Knishioner Eric Pavony, Schlegel, Erika & M, Princess Erin & The Baron, Eve, Kit & Baby Ruth, 5 deutsche Jungs in Florenz, The Jacobs, The Rafilsons, Sehorn, Ian & Lizzo and Eugene & Jacki and The Mapps, Veeves, Greggy, Haley, Holly, Kashinsky, James Gregg, J$, Jenny, Newton, Josh, Joshua, JUDY!, Jules & Zoe, Just In Kase, Rand & Kaiju Big Battel, Kelly West, German + Slaby, Kevin Sullivan, the Kickstarter community, Klaus und meine alten Freunde vom Kehrer Verlag, LJ, Linda, Lindsey, Krantzy Pants, Conran & his mum Liz, Lukas, Maria, Mara, Maeve, Matia & TomPatt, Eich, MMM, Cousin Matt, OlsonFarlow, m, Anna & Scout, Wichita, Mishka & Scott, Kepka, Pancho, The Eshelmans, PFal, House Pendergast, The fun(ny) Getzlaffs, Gauthier, Cousin Rob, Hoots & the bubs, The Mattsons, Lewkowicz, Scottys Mac and Mazariegos, Strazz, Mom & Rob, Bittle, Bates & Sweet Stella Bee, Sheila & Sherman, Bags, The Sue, ™ (RMFT!) & Patrick (War Beagle!), Tara & Eric, TBrown, Vince, Viv și Cata, Braco Vragovic and Yooners. I'd also like to personally thank ________________.

I am so grateful to have reconnected with Barker, a beautiful, talented, and hilarious woman. What a gift to share time and space with someone who, for some reason, truly understands and appreciates this complicated weirdo. Thanks to you and Dills for all your love.

A special thank you to my incredibly talented photo editor, Mike Davis, for encouraging me to pursue and cherish adjectives and adverbs in my photography.

I can't believe how many times I've leaned on Tanyia Johnson to bail me out with her intelligent and graceful graphic design skills. (Trust me, she can't either.) Once again, TJ has saved my ass. I so appreciate you.

And a shoutout to Chuck, who has looked over ALL THE WORDS and with amazing skill and intuition inserted ALL THE DAD JOKES I meant to include.

Tamika, who ever thought we'd make it this far, homie?

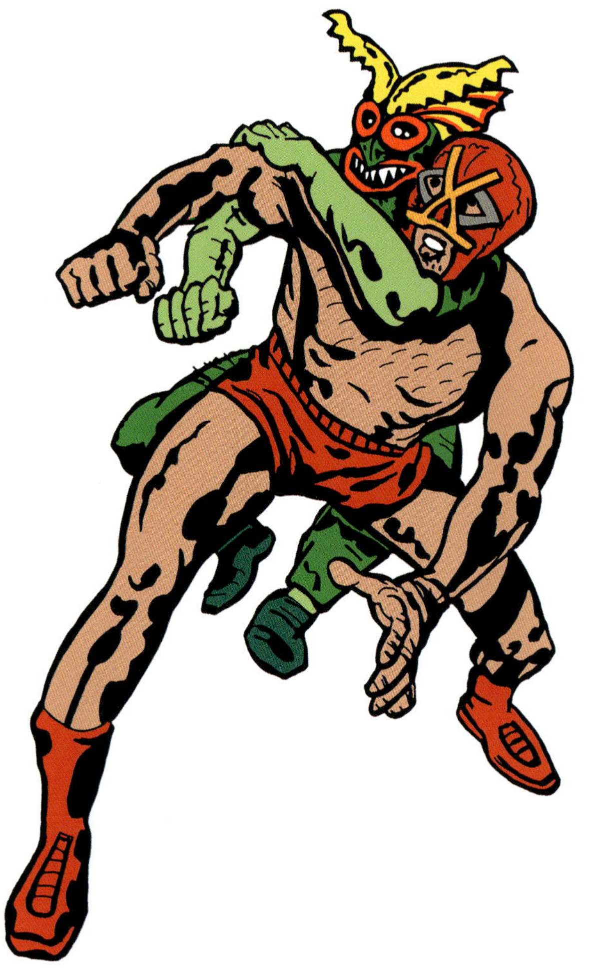

I never thought I'd ever have a photobook published, let alone three. Are you kidding? Yet, here we are. As Cousin Rob would say, I'm so goddamn lucky.

Everyone wants to be seen and heard, understood and appreciated. Every. Single. Person. That's especially true of every artist. Sadly, that doesn't always happen. But when it does, you cherish the experience and hold it close to your heart forever.

That's how I feel about meeting Alexa Becker.

Back in 2010, I traveled to Frankfurt to attend the world's largest book fair. I had an ambitious and, frankly, unrealistic goal: Find a book publisher for my ongoing photo project on sports culture. Yeah, I know, total long shot. I figured, at worst, it was a great chance to see my German buddy Peter for pivo and laughs.

Packing a book dummy I'd made with Mike Davis, determination and a helluva lot of naïveté, I wandered around the vast halls looking for a connection to any publisher who printed photobooks. Let's just say I found more demand for nudes by dead celebrity photographers than what I happened to be offering. But then I came across an elegant yet subtle display of gorgeous and stylish photobooks by the publishing house Kehrer Verlag. That's where I met Alexa, who helped choose what Kehrer would publish.

I introduced myself, told her a bit about my work, which included some Weird Sports. "Oh, I think I know your work," she told me. I found that impossible. No one knew of my Weird Sports work, not then, and definitely not a European editor. Then she asked, "Didn't your dad die when you were a kid?" Thankfully, the ground was there to catch my jaw.

Turns out, Alexa sat on the jury for a photobook contest I'd entered earlier that year. While I didn't win, let alone make the final round, she remembered my work and my mission statement, which mentioned how important sports was to me while growing up without a father. To this day, I remain stunned she remembered me.

Alexa was the first and only person that day to look at my book from beginning to end, appreciating not just the images of people at play but also the intention and sequencing. I left feeling excited, and a little confused. Alexa had offered me a letter of intent, whatever the hell that was. (Later, I found out it meant Kehrer agreed to publish my work.) Despite my confusion, I knew something important happened. I grabbed a hefeweizen and celebrated by myself at the biergarten.

It's a large reason why I love this bookmaking process, why it's so important to me. It's not just that I found a publisher to make my weird books, I found a team of kühl humans I connect with.

Thank you Alexa and Kehrer Verlag for making me feel seen and heard, understood and appreciated.

Sol Neelman (born 1970) is a failed prep athlete turned sports photographer from the wonderfully weird suburbs of Portland, Oregon.

After squeaking by with a journalism degree at the University of Oregon (Go Ducks!), Sol launched his photography career in 1996 with a humanitarian agency in what was then called Yugoslavia. The following year, Sol returned to Oregon and landed a gig with the community paper in McMinnville. In 2000, he split to photograph for the Beaver State's largest paper, *The Oregonian*. He was part of the team that won a Pulitzer for the paper's Breaking News Reporting, right before exiting for a freelance career in 2007.

Since then, Sol has traveled the world chronicling some of the weirdest sports on Earth. In that time he has cheated death on a 60-foot forklift, been knocked unconscious by a bronco at a prison rodeo, and tumbled off a ski lift overloaded with furries. Oh, he also covered the Olympics once or twice.

Sol's work has graced the pages of pretty much every publication worth reading, from *National Geographic* to *ESPN* to *The New York Times*. It even appeared in *Penthouse* (long story), which is probably better than Sol appearing in *Penthouse*. Advertising clients include one or two companies you might know of, including *Nike*, *adidas*, and *Clif Bar*. This is his third *Weird Sports* photobook published by world-renowned fine art book publisher *Kehrer Verlag*. (Danke, Klaus!)

This book is
dedicated to my
brother Bart (#52)

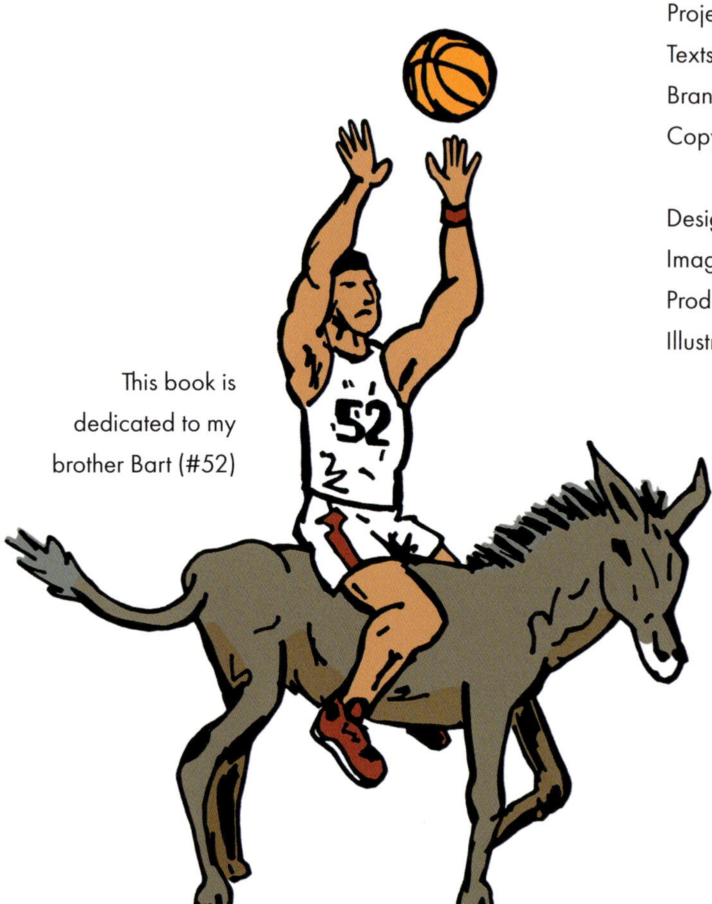

Photo Editor: Mike Davis
Project Management: Kehrer Verlag (Aydria Stadter)
Texts: David Noles, Cousin Rob Hart, Sol Neelman,
Brandy Rettig
Copy Editor: Chuck Squatriglia

Design: Tanyia Johnson and Kehrer Design (Katha Stumpf)
Image Processing: Kehrer Design (Patrick Horn)
Production Management: Kehrer Design (Tom Streicher)
Illustrations: Rand Borden

Printed and bound in Germany
ISBN 978-3-96900-113-4

Kehrer Heidelberg
www.kehrerverlag.com